Praise for
The More of Less

"I'm so inspired by this wise, timely book! Like so many people right now, I'm drawn to the idea of minimalism, but, to be honest, I find myself pretty deeply entrenched in bad habits of clutter and accumulation. I'm so thankful for Joshua's clear vision for what life can be when we choose to surround ourselves with less stuff, and how in doing so, we create more space for living and dreaming."

—SHAUNA NIEQUIST, author of *Bread & Wine* and *Savor*

"Joshua Becker is a distinguished voice in the modern minimalism movement. Engaging and nonjudgmental, *The More of Less* masterfully articulates the benefits—and the joy—of living with less."

—JOSHUA FIELDS MILLBURN, creator of theminimalists.com and coauthor of *Everything That Remains*

"Joshua Becker is one of my heroes. If you're struggling with too much stuff and too little happiness, here is your must-read."

—PETER WALSH, *New York Times* best-selling author of *It's All Too Much*

"Joshua Becker reveals an innovative approach that adds more meaning to our schedules, personal well-being, relationships, finances, and passions. Don't let the word *minimalist* intimidate you. There are no drastic measures required, and no set plans you must follow. Open this book to unburden your life and give oxygen to what matters most."

—RACHEL MACY STAFFORD, *New York Times* best-selling author of *Hands Free Mama* and *Hands Free Life*

"I've enjoyed Joshua Becker's message and writing for many years, and this is by far his best work. His very practical advice for living with less, together with moving stories from real people living with less, provides the tools and motivation for powerful change. I'm in awe of how Becker weaves the step-by-step *how to* with the moving *why to* of minimalism."

— COURTNEY CARVER, author of *Simple Ways to Be More with Less*

"This is it—the book that will change your life with a surprisingly simple solution: Less can actually mean more. A whole lot more."

—JEFF GOINS, best-selling author of *The Art of Work*

"Joshua Becker leads you through the steps of finding the life you want by getting to the heart of what you need. If you have been looking for a practical, actionable guide to help you find a simpler and more fulfilling way of living, this is it."

—PATRICK RHONE, author of *enough*

"This definitive book on minimalism offers the 'why,' the 'how,' and the 'who.' Because Joshua is a longtime practitioner with sound credibility, readers can rest assured that whatever steps they'll be taking will lead to a richer life of joy, generosity, meaning, and wholeness."

—RICHARD DAHLSTROM, senior pastor of Bethany Community
Church, Seattle, WA

"Often our biggest fear about living with less is that we might miss out, but Joshua Becker explains just how much we have to gain from the minimalist lifestyle. Packed with actionable ideas you can apply today, *The More of Less* is the perfect balance of instruction and motivation."

—RUTH SOUKUP, *New York Times* best-selling author of *Unstuffed*

"Joshua Becker is promoting a way to do life that is more than attractive— it's a really big idea that will radically change lives."

—JEFF SHINABARGER, founder of Plywood People and author of *More
or Less: Choosing a Lifestyle of Excessive Generosity*

"With amusing stories and practical advice, Joshua explains how to make your minimalist journey a group endeavor with friends and family."

—DAVE BRUNO, author of *The 100 Thing Challenge*

"I came to *The More of Less* a skeptic. By the end, though—thanks to Joshua Becker's gentle, simple, persuasive way of explaining things—I'd thrown out a bunch of stuff, and I was a convert."

—JAMES WALLMAN, author of *Stuffocation*

THE MORE
OF LESS

Finding the Life You Want
Under Everything You Own

JOSHUA BECKER

WATERBROOK
PRESS

THE MORE OF LESS
PUBLISHED BY WATERBROOK PRESS
12265 Oracle Boulevard, Suite 200
Colorado Springs, Colorado 80921

Hardcover ISBN 978-1-60142-796-0
eBook ISBN 978-1-60142-798-4

Published in the United States by WaterBrook Multnomah, an imprint of the Crown Publishing Group, a division of Penguin Random House LLC, New York.

WATERBROOK® and its deer colophon are registered trademarks of Penguin Random House LLC.

Library of Congress Cataloging-in-Publication Data
Names: Becker, Joshua, author.
Title: The more of less : finding the life you want under everything you own / Joshua Becker.
Description: First Edition. | Colorado Springs, Colorado : WaterBrook Press, 2016. | Includes bibliographical references.
Identifiers: LCCN 2015042586 (print) | LCCN 2015043638 (ebook) | ISBN 9781601427960 (hard cover) | ISBN 9781601427984 (electronic)
Subjects: LCSH: Simplicity—Religious aspects—Christianity. | Consumption (Economics)—Religious aspects—Christianity.
Classification: LCC BV4647.S48 B43 2016 (print) | LCC BV4647.S48 (ebook) | DDC 241/.68—dc23
LC record available at http://lccn.loc.gov/2015042586

Printed in the United States of America
2016—First Edition

10 9 8 7 6 5 4 3 2 1

Dedicated to the entire Becoming Minimalist community. Your support and encouragement have served as an inspiration to me and made this book possible. May your lives continue to inspire others to live more by owning less.

Contents

Becoming Minimalist

In 2008, Memorial Day weekend promised to deliver beautiful weather—not always the case in Vermont at that time of year. So my wife, Kim, and I decided to spend that Saturday shopping, running errands, and catching up on chores. Spring cleaning was our big goal for the weekend, starting with the garage.

Saturday morning dawned, and as Kim and our infant daughter slept on, I got our son, Salem, out of bed early for some eggs and bacon. I thought that after a nice breakfast he might be in a state of mind to help his dad. Looking back now, I'm not sure why I thought a five-year-old would feel eager about cleaning a garage, but nevertheless this was my hope. After breakfast we made our way to it.

Our two-car garage, as always, was full of stuff. Boxes stacked one on top of another threatened to fall off shelves. Bikes were tangled together, leaned against a wall. A garden hose slumped in loops in a corner. Rakes and shovels and brooms leaned every which way. Some days we'd have to turn sideways when getting in and out of our cars to squeeze through the mess that filled the garage.

"Salem," I said, "here's what we need to do. This garage has gotten dirty and messy over the winter, so we're going to pull everything out onto the driveway. Then we're going to hose down the entire garage, and after it's dry, we'll put everything back more organized. Okay?"

The little guy nodded, pretending to understand everything I had just told him.

I motioned to a plastic bin in the corner and asked Salem to drag it out.

Unfortunately, this particular bin happened to be full of Salem's summer toys. As you can imagine, as soon as my son was reunited with toys he hadn't seen in months, the last thing he wanted to do was help me clean the garage. He grabbed his Wiffle ball and bat and began heading for the backyard.

On his way out, he stopped. "Will you play with me, Dad?" he asked, a hopeful expression on his face.

"Sorry, buddy. I can't," I told him. "But we can play as soon as I finish. I promise."

With a pang, I watched Salem's brown head disappear around the corner of the garage.

As the morning crept along, one thing led to another, and the possibility that I would be able to join Salem in the backyard began to look less and less likely. I was still working in the garage hours later when Kim called Salem and me in for lunch.

When I headed back outside to finish the job, I noticed our next-door neighbor June working in her own yard, planting flowers and watering her garden. June was an elderly woman with gray hair and a kindly smile who had always taken an interest in my family. I waved to her and got on with my work.

By this point, I was trying to clean and organize all the stuff I had dragged out of the garage in the morning. It was hard work and taking much longer than I had expected. As I worked, I thought about all the times lately that I had been feeling discontented while taking care of our stuff. Here was yet another time! What made it worse was that Salem kept appearing from the backyard to ask questions or try to convince me to play with him. Each time I'd tell him, "Almost done, Salem."

June could recognize the frustration in my body language and tone of voice. At one point, as we happened to pass each other, she said to me sarcastically, "Ah, the joys of home ownership." She had spent most of the day caring for her own home.

I responded, "Well, you know what they say—the more stuff you own, the more your stuff owns you."

Her next words changed the course of my life. "Yeah," she said, "that's why my daughter is a minimalist. She keeps telling me I don't need to own all this stuff."

I don't need to own all this stuff.

The sentence reverberated in my mind as I turned to look at the fruits of my morning labor: a large pile of dirty, dusty possessions stacked in my driveway. Suddenly, out of the corner of my eye, I noticed my son, alone in the backyard, still playing by himself. The juxtaposition of the two scenes dug deep into my heart, and I began to recognize the source of my discontent for the first time.

It was piled up in my driveway.

I already knew that possessions don't equal happiness. Doesn't everybody? At least we all profess to know that our things won't bring us true satisfaction. But in that moment, as I surveyed the pile of stuff in my driveway, another realization came to me: *Not only are my possessions not bringing happiness into my life; even worse, they are actually distracting me from the things that do!*

I ran inside the house and found my wife upstairs scrubbing a bathtub. Still trying to catch my breath, I said, "Kim, you'll never guess what just happened. June said we don't need to own all this stuff!"

And in that moment a minimalist family was born.

A New Calling

That weekend, Kim and I started talking about what we could get rid of to simplify our lives and return our focus to what really mattered to us. We began selling, giving away, and throwing away things we didn't need. Within six months, we had gotten rid of 50 percent of our belongings. We quickly began seeing the benefits of minimalism and developing a philosophy for how simpler, more purposeful living is something everyone can benefit from.

I was so excited about it that by the end of Memorial Day weekend, I had created a blog—called *Becoming Minimalist*—to keep our extended family up to date with our journey. It began as nothing more than an online journal for me. But then something amazing happened: people I didn't know began reading the blog and telling their friends about it. My readers grew into the hundreds, then the thousands, then the tens of thousands . . . and the numbers just kept growing.

I kept thinking, *What is going on here? What does this mean?*

For years, I had been a student-ministry pastor at various

churches. In Vermont, our student ministry was the largest of any church in New England. I loved helping middle-school and high-school students find greater spiritual meaning for their lives. Nevertheless, I began to sense that this minimalism blog played some role in my life's destiny.

I began receiving e-mails with specific questions about owning less, inquiries from media outlets, and speaking requests. Promoting minimalism became a deep and enduring passion for me. I realized this was an important message—one that could help people of all backgrounds and all spiritual persuasions, living all over the world, to better their lives. Perhaps I needed to promote minimalism full time, I thought.

As an experimental transition, in 2012 I agreed to move to Arizona and spend two years helping a friend start a church, while at the same time laying the foundation for a new career. At the end of those two years, I made the transition to full-time promoter of the benefits of owning less.

Today, the blog is going stronger than ever, with readership now in excess of one million readers every month. I have also published a subscription newsletter and some books. More and more these days, I am asked to speak at sustainability conferences, professional-organizing chapter meetings, entrepreneurial events, Christian conferences, and other gatherings. The opportunities to share about minimalism continue to increase.

I have learned a lot about minimalism in the years since my garage-cleaning experience. The best of my discoveries appear here in *The More of Less*. Yet the point I will keep coming back to is the same insight I had on that first day: Our excessive possessions are not making us happy. Even worse, they are taking us away from the things that do. Once we let go of the things that don't matter, we are free to pursue all the things that really do matter.

This is a message desperately needed in a society heavily motivated by the possibility of owning large amounts of stuff. And I believe it is a message that will bring you new life and greater joy.

What Your Closets Are Telling You

Will Rogers once said, "Too many people spend money they haven't earned to buy things they don't want to impress people they don't like." [1] His analysis is truer today than when he first uttered it. It's true, I suspect, in all the wealthier nations of the world. But let me take my own country—the United States of America—as an example.

In America, we consume twice as many material goods as we did fifty years ago. [2] Over the same period, the size of the average American home has nearly tripled, and today that average home contains about three hundred thousand items. [3] On average, our homes contain more televisions than people. [4] And the US Department of Energy reports that, due to clutter, 25 percent of people with two-car garages don't have room to park cars inside and another 32 percent have room for only one vehicle. [5] Home organization, the service that's trying to find places for all our clutter, is now an $8 billion industry, growing at a rate of 10 percent each year. [6] And still one out of every ten American households rents off-site storage—the fastest-growing segment of the commercial real-estate industry over the past four decades. [7]

No wonder we have a personal-debt problem. The average household's credit-card debt stands at over $15,000, while the average mortgage debt is over $150,000.[8]

I'll stop there with the statistics dump, because I don't want to depress you. Besides, you don't need statistics and surveys to help you recognize that you very likely own too much stuff. You see it as you walk through your house every day. Your living space has become filled with possessions of every kind. Your floor space is crowded. Your closets are stuffed. Your drawers are overflowing. Even your freezer can't hold all the food you want to put in it. And there never seems to be enough cabinet space.

Am I right?

Although you probably sort of like most of the stuff you own, I suspect that, nevertheless, you have a sense that it's just too much and you want to do something about it. But how do you know what to keep and what to get rid of? How do you go about removing unneeded stuff from your life? When will you know that you've reached the right level of accumulation?

You may have picked up this book hoping for ideas about decluttering your house. You'll get them, I promise. And so much more as well! I'm going to show you how to find the life you want hidden under all the stuff you own. It's a "less is more" message with an emphasis on the *more*.

The payoff isn't just a clean house—it's a more satisfying, more meaningful life. Minimalism is an indispensable key to the better life you've been searching for all along.

I'll be honest with you. Deep down, I have a big dream for this book: I want to introduce the world to minimalism. On average, at least in my own country, we see five thousand ads every day telling us to buy more.[9] I want to be a voice urging us to buy less, because the potential benefits for our world are incalculable when hundreds, thousands, millions of lives are transformed by minimalism.

THE UNIVERSAL BENEFITS OF MINIMALISM

There is more joy to be found in owning less than can ever be found in pursuing more. In a world that constantly tells us to buy more and more, we often lose sight of that. But consider the life-giving benefits. You can expect a payoff in every one of the following areas if you practice the principles of minimalism taught in *The More of Less*.

- *More time and energy*—Whether we are making the money to buy them, researching and purchasing them, cleaning and organizing them, repairing them, replacing them, or selling them, our possessions consume our time and energy. So the fewer things we have, the more of our time and energy we'll have left to devote to other pursuits that matter more to us.

- *More money*—It's simple enough: By buying fewer things, we spend less money. Not just to acquire things in the first place but also to manage and maintain our goods. Maybe your path to financial freedom comes not from earning more but from owning less.

- *More generosity*—Living a less acquisitive, less costly lifestyle provides the opportunity to financially support causes we care about. Our money is only as valuable as what we choose to spend it on, and there are countless opportunities worth vastly more than material accumulation.

- *More freedom*—Excess possessions have the power to enslave us physically, psychologically, and financially. Stuff is cumbersome and difficult to transport. It weighs on the spirit and makes us feel heavy. On the other hand, every time we remove an unnecessary item, we gain back a little freedom.

- *Less stress*—Every added possession increases the worry in our lives. In your mind, imagine two rooms: one that is cluttered and messy, and another that is tidy and sparse. Which one makes you feel anxious? Which one makes you feel calm? Mess + excess = stress.

- *Less distraction*—Everything around us competes for our attention. These small distractions can add up and prevent us from giving attention to the things we care about. And these days, who needs more distraction?

- *Less environmental impact*—Overconsumption accelerates the destruction of natural resources. The less we consume, the less damage we do to our environment, and that benefits everyone, including our children's and grandchildren's generations.

- *Higher-quality belongings*—The less money you spend on an excess quantity of things, the greater your opportunity to purchase quality possessions when you need them. Minimalism is not necessarily the same as frugality. It is a philosophy recognizing that owning more stuff is not better; owning better stuff is better.

- *A better example for our kids*—What is the most common three-word phrase our children hear from us? Is it "I love you"? Or is it "I want that," "It's on sale," or "Let's go shopping"? It's important to give our children a framework with which to counteract the out-of-control lifestyle marketed to them.

- *Less work for someone else*—If we don't make the effort to sort through and pare down our possessions, then when we die or get to the point where we can't take care of ourselves anymore, someone else (probably a loved one) is going to have to take up that burden. By sticking to the minimalist path, we make it easier for the other person.

- *Less comparison*—Our natural tendencies cause us to compare our lives with those around us. Combine that with the fact that we seem to have a built-in desire to impress others by owning as much as possible, then as Will Rogers said, we've got a recipe for disaster. Purposefully owning less begins to take us out of the unwinnable game of comparison.

- *More contentment*—We tend to think that we can resolve our discontentment by getting the item whose lack is seemingly making us unhappy. Yet material possessions will never fully satisfy the desires of our hearts. (That's

why discontentment always returns after a purchase.)
Only after we intentionally break the cycle of accumulating more, more, more can we begin to discern the true causes of discontentment in our lives.

More time, more money, less stress, less distraction, more freedom. It all sounds appealing, doesn't it? You'll be hearing more about these themes in the rest of the book, where I'll show you how to make these universal benefits your own.

Even if these universal benefits were the only reasons for practicing minimalism, they would be enough. But there's more. There's also the *personalized* benefit each of us can get from minimalism. Getting rid of what you don't need is the first step toward crafting the life you want.

FULFILLING YOUR GREATEST PASSIONS

When we embrace minimalism, we are immediately freed to pursue our greatest passions. And for some of us, it's been a long time since we've had access to the resources required to chase our hearts' greatest delights—however we define those delights. Living with less offers more time to spend on meaningful activities, more freedom to travel, more clarity in our spiritual pursuits, increased mental capacity to solve our most heartfelt problems, healthier finances to support causes we believe in, and greater flexibility to pursue the careers we most desire.

For me, one passion I have been freed up to pursue is inviting others to discover the benefits of the minimalist lifestyle. In many ways, I feel like I get to play the neighbor role in others' lives. I am thankful that June introduced me to minimalism, and I am thankful that I have opportunities to pass it on to others.

Another big part of what I have personally gained from minimalism is better relationships. I love having more leisure time to spend with my immediate family, my extended family, and my friends. I also still participate regularly in my church, volunteering to do many of the things I used to do as a church employee. At the same time, I am free to pursue my relationship with God with less distraction and more freedom, and that means everything to me.

Recently, I have been very excited that, through the profits from this book, my wife and I have been able to create a nonprofit organization called The Hope Effect. Its mission is to change how the world cares for orphans by establishing a reproducible model of orphan care that mimics the family unit. When we had the idea for this nonprofit, Kim and I said to each other, "Why not? Let's do something meaningful with our resources." Because our financial obligations are modest, we were able to go for it. I'll be telling you more about this project later in the book.

My life is proof: subtracting unneeded stuff multiplies opportunities to pursue things you care about. The result is exponential growth in personal satisfaction. Maybe the life you've always wanted is buried under everything you own!

So let me ask you, what are your greatest unfulfilled passions? What might you have the potential to enjoy, pursue, or complete if you minimize your possessions? Do you want to connect more deeply with loved ones? See the world? Create art? Improve your physical fitness? Achieve financial security? Give yourself to a big cause?

Keep those dreams in mind while you're reading, because that is really what this book is about. It's not just about owning less stuff. It's about living a bigger life!

WHAT TO EXPECT

I hope you are excited about the possibilities that this book represents. I have much more to say to you, both about the philosophy and the practicalities of minimalism. I believe this is the kind of book you will look back on later and think, *That book changed my life forever!* And I hope it is one you will pass along to others when you finish it.

To be clear, this book is not a memoir about my own journey in minimalism. Although I will share some of my own story along the way to illustrate what I am saying and hopefully provide inspiration, the book isn't about me. It's about you. It's about the joys of owning less. It's about how to implement minimalism in a way that transforms your life for the better.

I will also be introducing you to other people who have become minimalists and today intentionally own less. Many of them have been in situations that you will recognize from your own life, and what they did about their consumeristic habits will give you inspiration and ideas for embarking on a minimalist journey of your own. For example, you will learn about . . .

- Troy, for whom chipped paint on a windowsill started an adventure in minimalism

- Annette, who decided not to own a home at all, preferring to travel the world
- Dave and Sheryl, who saw creative and charitable desires bubble up inside themselves when they minimized
- Margot, who amazed herself by getting rid of one thousand items from her home
- Courtney, who has slowed the progress of a life-threatening disease by de-stressing her life
- Ryan, who packed every single thing he owned in boxes, then took out only what he needed
- Sarah, who changed her shopping habits forever by refusing to buy new clothes for an entire year
- Jessica, who developed her own minimalist philosophy starting when she was fifteen
- Ali, who gave up her most precious piece of jewelry—and changed the lives of people on the other side of the world because of it

You'll notice too that I will mention some stories from the Bible. My religious background has played a significant role in both my understanding and my practice of minimalism. You'll see me make the connection periodically throughout the book.

If you are from a different faith or a nonfaith background, I think you will find these stories both interesting and helpful. They highlight and illustrate some universal truths about life and the world around us. It won't take you long to recognize why I chose to include them.

Based on my experiences in meeting people all over the world and talking about the benefits of owning less, I don't have any hesitation in affirming that minimalism is a way of life that can be transforming for everybody, everywhere. Keep reading *The More of Less* and let me prove it to you. Like a seed, its message is so simple and so full of the promise of growth.

RIGHT AROUND THE CORNER

I remember the Saturday of Labor Day weekend in 2008. It was a day with clear skies and warm weather, similar to that day three months earlier when I had gotten so frustrated while cleaning out our garage. This day, however, Kim and I had very little housework to do. Although we weren't yet finished minimizing, already we had reduced our possessions to a point where we didn't have to work around the house nearly as much as we used to. So our family was free to spend the day together doing the things we enjoyed. We wandered the wooded trails near our home, enjoyed a leisurely lunch on our porch, and pushed our kids on the swings.

Early that evening, I headed with Salem to the quiet street in front of our home. He was learning to ride his bike, and I was as proud as a father can be, straightening his helmet, giving him pushes to get started, and running up and down the street to make sure he stayed upright. I was pleased to see that he was really getting the hang of this new skill.

Before we finished, I challenged Salem to ride his bike all the way around the block without any help. I would go with him on my own bike—our first bicycle ride together.

As we turned the corner, I observed a neighbor in his driveway, looking tired, exasperated, and frustrated . . .

. . . cleaning out his garage!

I smiled to myself.

Someday, when the time was right, I would have a life-changing message for him: you don't need to own all that stuff.

2

Good Riddance

What do you think of when you hear the word *minimalism*?

If you're like many people, it may conjure up images of sterility, of asceticism, of bare white walls, of grim frugality, or of someone sitting on the floor because he doesn't have any furniture. It might seem to you like an exercise in self-deprivation simply for the sake of self-deprivation. How boring and colorless! Who would want that?

But let me tell you . . . this view is *so far* from what I mean by minimalism!

To me, minimalism is exactly the opposite. It speaks to me of freedom, of peace, and of joy. It's about space that has been opened up to make room for new possibilities. It's truly "good riddance" because it clears away obstacles to the lives we want to live.

I'm not so much interested in minimalism, per se, as I am in helping people get to the level of possessions that will enable them to live the best lives they're capable of. For those of us living in the more developed nations of the world, about 98 percent of the time this means reducing our possessions, not increasing them. Therefore, as a practical matter, we have to learn the skill of minimizing.

With that as a background, here is my definition.

MINIMALISM: the intentional promotion of the things we
most value and the removal of anything that distracts us from
them

The beauty of minimalism isn't in what it takes away. The beauty
and the full potential of minimalism lie in what it gives.

Troy Koubsky would certainly agree.

A BIRTH OF HOPE

"The reason I am a minimalist today," Troy began, "is because of the
color of my house."

I'd never heard that one before, so I asked Troy to explain what
he meant. Troy was a tall man of about forty with red hair and a red
beard cropped close. The two of us were at a simple-living conference
in Minneapolis when he shared his story.

Troy explained that, a few years earlier, he had bought a house
with the understanding that his friend would move in and help with
the payments. But then, because of a change in life circumstances, the
friend moved out. Rather than try to find a new roommate, Troy
opted to take a second job and increase his income to support the
home all on his own.

"Eventually," he said, "the situation began to take a toll on me. I
had more money but less time. And to make matters worse, I was not
able to save any of the excess income. It was practically all going into
the mortgage payment."

Troy entered a season of despair. He began to buy and collect things to satisfy his craving for a sense of control. Garage sales and clearance end caps became his drugs of choice. Looking back, he says, "I was out of control, totally numb to what I was doing to myself and my living space. Until I noticed the paint on my window trim beginning to chip."

In preparation for the window repair, Troy opened his browser during a lunch break at work and searched for paint colors. The search returned so many color choices that at first he felt paralyzed.

As he scrolled down, however, he happened to notice one image on the screen that did not look like the others. It showed the smallest house he had ever seen, just a few hundred square feet—a Tiny House on wheels, with chickens in the front yard.

Troy was intrigued. With just a few clicks, he was immersed in a world of people purposely living in smaller homes with less stuff. It was the start of Troy's journey to minimalism.

His immediate goal was to make his existing home more livable. Over the next month, Troy removed 1,389 things from his home. By the end of the summer, the number of items he had removed totaled more than 3,000 items.

"It has not always been easy to let go of stuff," Troy told me, "but it is a process I want and I need."

He ended our conversation with tears in his eyes. "I was really hurting for a long time, Joshua. I needed simplicity. I needed to get out of debt. I needed to get rid of the stuff cluttering up my life. But mostly I needed hope—hope that life could be different, better. This process of becoming minimalist and living with less has given it to me."

There it is: Minimalism is about what it gives, not what it takes away. It's the intentional promotion of the things we most value and the removal of anything that distracts us from them. It's a new way of living that fills us with hope.

With that perspective firmly in mind, let me try to clear up two common misconceptions about minimalism.

Misconception 1: Minimalism Is About Giving Up Everything

Curiously to me, some people seem to think that minimizing means throwing out everything or, at any rate, almost everything. That's not the case at all. Rather, minimalism is about living with less, and as I often say, less is not the same as none.

If you were to walk into my home today, you would probably not immediately assume that a minimalist family lives there. In our living room, you would find seating for four, a family photo, a rug, a coffee table, and our only television. In our coat closet, you would find jackets, baseball caps, and a few winter-weather accessories. In our kids' rooms, you would find books, craft supplies, and toys in the closets.

We are seeking to live a minimalist life, but at the same time we are still living, breathing, changing human beings. To live is to consume. So we still have possessions. But we have worked hard to escape the *excessive* accumulation of possessions.

I sometimes talk about "rational minimalism" or "strategic minimalism" to get at what I mean. I don't advocate getting rid of everything humanly possible. Instead, I encourage people to get rid of what isn't necessary so they can better pursue their goals in life.

I am passionate about my soul, about my family, and about

loving and influencing others. I focus on these priorities above everything else. Minimalism is a means to these ends for me. It removes physical distractions so I can realize my greatest priorities. So I ruthlessly get rid of what I have to in order to be true to my objectives. But if there are things that help me live my life the way I need to, I keep them and enjoy them. I don't feel guilty about them at all.

It can be the same for you as you choose to walk down the path of minimalism. Don't make the mistake of thinking you have to live with nothing. Live with whatever possessions give you the life you want.

Misconception 2: Minimalism Is About Organizing Your Stuff

Organizing has its place. But it's not the same as minimizing.

Think about it. Organizing our stuff (without removing the excess) is only a temporary solution. We have to repeat it over and over. As my fellow minimalist Courtney Carver puts it, "If organizing your stuff worked, wouldn't you be done by now?"

At its heart, organizing is simply rearranging. And though we may find storage solutions today, we will be forced to find new ones as early as tomorrow. Additionally, organizing our stuff (without removing it) has some major shortcomings:

- *Organizing doesn't benefit anyone else.* The possessions we rarely use sit on shelves in our basements, attics, and garages, providing no benefit even while other people around us could use them.
- *Organizing doesn't solve our debt problems.* It never addresses the underlying issue that we buy too much stuff.

In fact, many times, the act of rearranging our stuff costs us even more as we purchase containers, storage units, or larger homes to house it.

- *Organizing doesn't turn back our desire for more.* The act of organizing our things into boxes, plastic bins, or extra closets is all about holding on to our excess accumulation. As such, it rarely thwarts our culture-driven inclination to find happiness in our possessions.

- *Organizing doesn't force us to evaluate our lives.* While rearranging our stuff may cause us to look at each of our possessions, it does not force us to ask ourselves whether we need to keep them. Too often, we just stuff them in boxes and close the lids, forgetting them once again.

- *Organizing accomplishes little in paving the way for other changes.* Organizing may provide a temporary lift to our attitudes because it results in a tidier room, but it rarely constitutes an actual lifestyle change. In our minds, our house is still too small, our income is still too little, and we still can't find enough time in the day. We may have rearranged our stuff, but not our lives.

By contrast, the act of removing possessions from our homes accomplishes many of these skipped-over purposes. It changes our hearts and changes our lives. Furthermore, it is a permanent solution, not a temporary one we have to repeat. Once we have removed an item, it is gone for good.

Organizing is better than nothing. But minimizing is better by far.

HISTORY SPEAKS

Finding the life we want isn't about giving up everything. Nor is it about holding on to everything and just trying to organize it better. Instead, it's about reducing the number of our possessions to a level that sets us free.

I find it fascinating that the wisdom of the ages and the wisdom of the sages agree on the value of this approach to living.

When my wife and I began decluttering our home and removing the nonessentials, I would often remark to her, "This is fantastic. Owning less stuff is so freeing! I wonder why nobody ever told me about this before?"

Before long, though, I started to catch myself. Was it really that nobody had ever told me about minimalism before? Or was it that I just hadn't been listening?

In my head, I began recounting the sermons I had heard preached about the spiritual dangers of materialism. And beyond that, throughout my life, I had read and heard dozens of challenges to reject the empty promises of consumerism and to follow a way based on higher values.

I began to do research and discovered that minimalism is not a new movement at all. Whether specifically labeled as *minimalism* or not, it has been practiced and encouraged for thousands of years — well before our current society of mass-produced goods, well before suburbanization, and even well before the Industrial Revolution. Under all kinds of economic conditions, minimalism has been promoted as a rewarding way of life.

Today, we recognize some of the people in recent centuries who have encouraged this approach to life, including Henry David Thoreau and John Ruskin. I even hear them referred to as the "fathers of the minimalist movement." But minimalism predates all of them—by a long shot. The minimalist lifestyle may be gaining in popularity today, but it is anything but new.

Duane Elgin, who is often credited with bringing the phrase *voluntary simplicity* into public discourse, said it to me like this: "I tell people that I'm the great-great-great-great-great-grandson of this movement that got started a couple of thousand years ago with the teachings of Jesus, Buddha, and other great sages who understood the value of simplicity. What is new is not the value of simplicity but rather the conditions of the world where it is understood."

Living with less has always been freeing and life giving, filling people with hope and purpose. It has enabled human beings to expand in spirit and to live as more than mere accumulators of possessions. And therefore minimalism is not a brand-new approach to life invented as a response to our overproduction of consumer goods. Quite the contrary. Our most trusted spiritual leaders have promoted it for centuries.

Including the person who has shaped my worldview more than any other: Jesus.

THE RICH YOUNG ANTI-MINIMALIST

At one point early in Jesus's teaching years, a young official approached him with a question that could hardly have been more weighty and consequential. "Good Teacher," he asked Jesus, "what must I do to deserve eternal life?"

Jesus's response came as a surprise and a shock to everyone. He said, "Sell everything you own and give it away to the poor. You will have riches in heaven. Then come, follow me."

The historian of this scene commented, "This was the last thing the official expected to hear. He was very rich and became terribly sad. He was holding on tight to a lot of things and not about to let them go."[1]

As I mentioned in the previous chapter, spirituality has shaped my pursuit and definition of minimalism. But minimalism has also shone a new light for me on some important spiritual teachings I have been familiar with for years. This one in particular.

You see, I used to read what Jesus said here about giving away possessions and money, then think, *That sounds like a recipe for a miserable life. Could that really be what he meant?* In a world that often defines happiness in terms of the amount of stuff we can accumulate, Jesus's instruction doesn't make sense. On good days, I would add this rationale: *Maybe if I sacrifice my stuff on earth today, I will receive rewards when I get to heaven. This must be the trade-off Jesus had in mind.*

But this thinking doesn't line up with other things Jesus said. For example, at one point Jesus stated, "I came so [you] can have real . . . life, more and better life than [you] ever dreamed of."[2] Jesus's teaching was always about getting the most out of every day of our lives on earth as well as into eternity.

However, as my family and I began to minimize our possessions and experience all of the benefits listed above, Jesus's words to the rich young official began to make new sense to me. Jesus was saying, "Sell your possessions and give to the poor because your things are an unnecessary burden to you! They are keeping you from experiencing the eternal, abundant life you are asking me about. Own less stuff. Your things are keeping you from becoming all that you were intended to become."

Jesus's instruction was not so much a test of the man's faith or a call to superhuman sacrifice as it was a statement of truth. It was an invitation to a better way of life. The man's possessions were keeping him from truly living!

This is a truth that people of every spiritual persuasion can embrace. To give you one example, I want to tell you about my friend Annette.

THE "ANYWHEREIST"

Annette Gartland is an Irish freelance journalist based mainly in Southeast Asia. She spends most of her time in Malaysia, travels frequently to Australia and Indonesia, goes to India when she can, visits Ireland and France once a year, and has plenty of other countries on her itinerary for the future.

It is minimalism, she says, that enables her to do all this. Annette has no permanent home and no car. She's been a web-working nomad since January 2013, when she decided to leave France. She calls herself an "anywhereist."

"After losing a significant job contract in 2009," she said to me, "I received some compensation and decided to go traveling. It was wonderful moving around with just a few bags. I would be away for three or four months and, each time I came home, I felt suffocated by all the stuff in my house and the cost of paying rent and bills and running a car."

That's when she decided to pare down her belongings to the minimum and become completely nomadic.

It took Annette three months of almost constant work to empty her home of accumulated belongings. (I've never said becoming minimalist is quick or easy!) She gave away most of her things, selling only a few high-tech items and some furniture and clothing.

As you might expect, Annette found some things harder to get rid of than others. "I still have several pairs of shoes stashed in boxes, and quite a few books and documents," she says. "Being minimalist doesn't mean giving everything away. It means only having things that we really need. And clearing is a process; it definitely takes time."

Additionally, *staying* minimalist is a day-to-day challenge for Annette. Things accumulate quickly. "When I go to events as a journalist," she says, "I am often given T-shirts or DVDs or books. I'm given calendars and all kinds of mementos." Sometimes Annette manages to pass on unwanted things to others right away, but other times she stuffs them in a bag that she sorts through when she can.

Traveling often involves a lot of organizing for Annette as she decides what to take with her on her next trip, but she sees the positive side of this labor. "There's great benefit in having to sort through my things regularly. I am keenly aware of everything I own and am forced to be honest about whether I need it or not."

Annette stays in hotels or does temporary apartment sharing, and sometimes she housesits. One of the main benefits of her way of life, she says, is having the time and energy to devote to developing her own environmental-news website, Changing Times.[3]

She testifies, "I see friends whose time and money are eaten up dealing with huge houses and gardens and managing their expensive lifestyles, and I am happy that I can focus on writing what I want to write. I also love being able to go wherever I like at the drop of a hat."

Now, I understand that your preferred lifestyle of less will look different from Annette's. In fact, minimalism is unique in each person's life. That's the subject we'll get to in the next chapter: how to live minimally in a way that is natural and appropriate for you.

But in every case, minimalism frees you up to live a better life. Isn't that what you want?

Regardless of what misconceptions you may have originally brought to the idea of minimalism, now you know the truth. Minimalism is the intentional promotion of the things we most value and the removal of anything that distracts us from them. It's for everyone who wants more out of less.

3

Minimalism Your Way

When I first started to research minimalism, I quickly discovered two things. First, there were a lot of people pursuing minimalism, far more than I'd had any notion of. This was a genuine movement underway all over the world, even though it mostly stayed beneath the radar. Second, the minimalists I found were doing minimalism in an amazing variety of ways.

- Dave Bruno limited his physical possessions to one hundred things while working at a university in San Diego. *Newsweek* picked up the story, and Dave's 100 Thing Challenge was becoming a growing trend among minimalists, one that would spawn even more drastic challenges (such as owning only 75, 50, or even 12 things).
- Colin Wright fit all his possessions in a backpack and moved to a new country every four months. To make the lifestyle even more interesting, he invited the readers of his website to vote on which country they would send him to next.
- Tammy Strobel lived with her husband and cat in a 128-square-foot home in Portland. The Strobels had

racked up over $30,000 in debt and embraced minimalist living as a means of overcoming it. But they fell so in love with the life that they continued living in a Tiny House even after they had retired their debt, becoming ambassadors for this housing option.

- Leo Babauta, a minimalist with six children, had recently moved from Guam to San Francisco with only the contents of one suitcase for each member of the family. Leo credits minimalism with helping him get out of debt, lose weight, stop smoking, and leave the job he couldn't stand.

In addition, Francine Jay, Everett Bogue, Karen Kingston, Adam Baker, and others shaped my early journey into minimalism.[1]

Each of these people and many more were singing the praises of their new lifestyle. I read them almost every day for inspiration. And it wasn't lost on me that all of them were accomplishing their goals in very different ways from one another.

Then I made the crucial step of applying this insight to myself.

Although there were many examples to follow if we wanted to, my wife and I didn't have to do minimalism in any particular way. There was no formula to follow, no standard to live up to. We were free to craft our own style of minimalism in any way that suited us. What a relief!

You might be feeling some relief too as you realize that you don't have to worry about anybody else's expectations of how you pursue a minimalist life. Perhaps at one time you were reluctant to try minimalism because you were afraid it would force you to do something you didn't want to do. But now you know that's an unnecessary fear.

Being a global nomad with no fixed address fits Annette Gartland (chapter 2) and Colin Wright just fine. But if that's not your dream, no problem.

If you have a feeling that your ideal number of possessions is quite a few more than one hundred, no problem.

If the thought of living in a Tiny House doesn't fit your goal in life, again, no problem!

You don't really need my permission, but if it helps, let me assure you that it's perfectly all right—and in fact desirable—for you to find your own individual path to a minimal lifestyle. That doesn't mean you won't be making big changes in your life. Probably you need to get rid of a lot of clutter in order to free yourself up. There's a big shake-up ahead. But it's going to be the particular kind of shake-up that *you* need, not one that somebody else needs. And you'll be glad when you do it.

It's not just that you're free to shape your personal approach to minimalism based upon your own *preferences*. More importantly, in this chapter I want to encourage you to shape your minimalism based upon your *purposes*. As best you can, identify the life you want to lead, and then pursue the kind of minimalism that will get you there.

Whatever we do, let's not start getting rigid about minimalism. It's easy enough to become doctrinaire, but staying focused on our purposes will keep us from falling into that trap.

IT DEPENDS

In the previous chapter, we looked at the incident where a rich young official approached Jesus with a question about eternal life. Jesus told him to sell everything he owned and give the proceeds to the poor.

I've known a lot of Christians who have looked at that story and tried to rationalize it away. "Jesus didn't *really* mean he was supposed to give it all away." (I'm sure there were times when I said the same thing myself.) We are so attached to our money and possessions that it's threatening to think about living without them.

On the other hand, some Christians throughout history (admittedly, a much smaller number) have looked at the story of the rich young official and have tried to apply it too broadly. They have thought that, to be faithful to God, people should give up practically everything they own. The only virtuous life, they have presumed, is one stripped of wealth, possessions, and even a home.

Both extremes—under-applying and over-applying Jesus's words—are mistakes. In fact, practicing minimalism has helped me to see that a one-size-fits-all mentality concerning possessions was far from Jesus's mind.

To explain, let me show you another incident from Jesus's life.

During his travels, Jesus came to an area called Gerasa and encountered one of life's tortured souls, a man afflicted by a mob of demons. The people living nearby feared him, so they tried to tie him up, but with his immense strength, he always broke free. No longer welcome among the living, he dwelt among the dead in the cemetery. From time to time, his cries would echo over the countryside. He would cut himself with stones. A sad, scary figure.

This man came up to Jesus, and Jesus had compassion on him, just as he did on the rich young official. Jesus cast out the demons. We can only imagine what awe and gratitude the man must have felt toward Jesus. At once, the man became peaceful. Since he had been wearing little or nothing, Jesus found a set of clothes for him.

Soon after, Jesus had to leave. The renewed man hated the thought of being separated from Jesus so soon. Other men, the twelve disciples, were traveling with Jesus; couldn't he do the same? "As Jesus was getting into the boat, the demon-delivered man begged to go along."

Note that this is exactly the reaction Jesus had wanted the rich young official to have! Jesus asked the official to sell everything and follow him. And in fact, when we read the Gospels, we see that Jesus routinely called people to leave everything and follow him. So wouldn't you think Jesus would say to the man from Gerasa, "Sure, hop in. I could use your help where we're going"?

But no, Jesus responded in a completely unexpected way, saying, "Go home to your own people. Tell them your story—what the Master did, how he had mercy on you."[2]

This contrast is important:

- In the story of the rich young official, Jesus said, "Sell everything you own and give it away to the poor. Then come, follow me."

- In the story of the homeless man from Gerasa, Jesus gave
  him a new set of clothes and then said, "Go back to your
  home. Tell them your story."

Let's ask ourselves, why did Jesus tell this second man to keep his
house, while he called the rich official and others to sell everything?

Answer: because they were called to fulfill different roles with
their lives. They were created for unique purposes.

We see a similar diversity of calling today among Christians.

It seems that God still calls some Christians to abandon everything. I think of Mother Teresa in Calcutta. Of Shane Claiborne, a
modern-day monastic in Philadelphia. Of Jan and Ellen Smit, who
left their home to start an orphanage for the daughters of women
prisoners in Thailand. All were motivated by their love for Christ.

But there are countless others who have received a different call.
They have been called to be farmers, bankers, writers, lawyers, or
schoolteachers. They were not called to abandon their homes for the
sake of the gospel. Just the contrary—like the man of Gerasa, they
were told to return to them!

If we are in this second category, does this mean we should buy
the biggest house our mortgage broker says we can afford and fill
every closet to overflowing? Of course not. We still find truth in Jesus's
words to the rich young ruler: excess possessions keep us from fulfilling our purpose. And surely we were created for something greater
than this!

Instead, we dream big dreams for our lives. We search for the greatest good we can accomplish with the one life we have been given. We
decipher what possessions we need to accomplish this role (a farmer, for

example, needs different supplies than a schoolteacher does). And then we refuse to allow anything to keep us from fulfilling our purpose.

Again, regardless of your spiritual worldview, you have dreams, you have passions about things you want to do, and you're tremendously concerned about the potential your future holds. This is why, for all of us, owning less is so important. It helps us do what we have been fitted to do, whatever that may be.

If necessary, we can figure out what that is on the fly.

HARNESS THE POWER OF HEURISTICS

Some people have a clear vision of what their purpose or goal in life is. For them, it's relatively easy to craft their individual form of minimalism. They just need to find a practice of minimalism that gives them the shortest path between where they are and where they hope to be.

Others—and I have no doubt it's the majority—are less clear about their objectives. They may have some inkling of what they want in life, but the picture of it in their minds is like a canvas that has only been partially brushed with paint. These people feel dissatisfaction with their overspending and overaccumulation, and they would like to make a change, but at the outset at least, they aren't able to fully map out what their approach to minimalism ought to be.

I was in this second category. You may be there too. If you have spent your entire life chasing things that don't matter, it could be difficult at first to recognize all the things that really do.

I want to encourage you to begin the process of minimizing anyway. I'm sure you have some excess possessions that you'll want to get rid of no matter what. As you do so, the process of minimizing will help to inform your vision for your future. Then your expanding vision of what you want will help to further refine your minimizing.

I think you'll find yourself asking questions like these: *Do I really need this object? Why or why not? What principles should be guiding what I keep and what I get rid of? What am I really going for here?*

It's not simply a top-down process of moving from goals to practice. Nor is it entirely a bottom-up process of figuring out how to own less as you go. It's both-and. You clarify your goals and settle into a less-encumbered lifestyle at the same time.

After my neighbor June told me I really *"didn't need to own all that stuff,"* Kim and I started getting rid of some of our things. But this brought us face to face with a lot of questions.

For example, one of the things cluttering up the garage was a set of golf clubs. I rarely used them. Would I really be playing golf much in the future? If not, was it worth keeping a set of clubs around? I decided golf was not a high priority of mine, so I got rid of the clubs.

But then we also had a dining table large enough for eight, with place settings for the same number, and yet we had a family of only four. Should we get a smaller table and give away half of our place settings? In this case, Kim and I decided we should not make those changes. We often had guests over or led groups from our church in our home, so being able to seat visitors at the table and feed them was important to us. In this case, the value of hospitality shaped our specific practice of minimalism.

In this way, minimizing became a *heuristical* process for us. That is, it was a learn-by-doing, learn-as-you-go experience. I recommend the same approach for everybody.

Get started on de-owning and decluttering right away. It will help you clarify your purpose and values. For example, it might become clearer to you that you want to spend less time on stuff so that you can spend more time with family and friends. Or once you start spending less money shopping, you may suddenly be freed up for a career change. Or you might realize that you want to get out of debt so that you can retire earlier, have money to travel, or be able to support causes you care about.

The specifics are as unique as you are. You'll find your way. Only you can do it, and you'll catch sight of your destination once you've begun the journey.

Ask my friends Dave and Sheryl Balthrop.

A ROAD TRIP TO MORE

In the spring of 2013, Dave and Sheryl took a long-overdue road trip, driving in their gray SUV from their home in Eugene, Oregon, down the beautiful coast of southern Oregon and California, as far as Santa Barbara.[3] For this couple, at last getting a break from their jobs and enjoying their new freedom as empty nesters, the trip was more than just a chance to relax and reconnect. It was also a time to focus on something that had been on their minds for a while: simplifying their lives. As images of the shining Pacific Ocean, dark forests, and grassy hillsides flashed by outside their car windows, they played podcasts and listened to the voices of minimalists talking about the value of owning less.

It was life transforming.

During this trip, the Balthrops went from flirting with the idea of minimizing to committing to it wholeheartedly.

This busy couple badly needed a change. Dave was a mentor to people with disabilities, and Sheryl was an attorney. Both were blessed with good health, challenging careers, and a loving family. But for a while they had felt they were increasingly coming up short. There was never enough time in the day or money in the bank.

Like most parents, they were committed to giving their kids the best life possible, as they saw it. They bought their dream home—a colonial-style house in Eugene—and borrowed against it over and over again to provide the comforts and luxuries of upper-middle-class America. But as their children began to graduate from high school and leave the nest, their nagging suspicion that something wasn't right continued to grow. Although they had sufficient financial resources, it was becoming increasingly difficult to find time for enjoying life with their family, planning for their future, and taking care of their health.

While listening to the podcasts on minimalism, they recognized a disconnect between what they claimed were their priorities and how they actually spent their time and resources. Sheryl said, "We realized that we continually deferred the things most important to us: spending time with family, giving, growing in our faith, taking care of our health, and setting aside sufficient funds for savings and retirement. We had sacrificed it all just to keep up our home and our appearance.

We were surprised to realize we had spent more time picking out the right couches for our living room than caring for our own health."

They resolved to take action and downsize their life. They sold off and gave away a large percentage of their stuff. And they moved into a much smaller home right across the street from their old place.

The result? After minimizing their possessions, Dave and Sheryl today celebrate a new life of decreased distraction. They are finally able to give priority to the things that matter most in their lives: their family, their faith, and their peace of mind.

But their story doesn't end there. You see, unburdened from caring for unnecessary belongings, Dave and Sheryl began to see new passions emerge in their lives. Dave discovered a love of writing. Sheryl began to recognize in herself a concern for families in need, eventually changing her entire law practice from litigation to mediation. Both have become more purposeful in creating for their children a legacy that extends beyond the size of their home.

The Balthrops were drawn to minimalism because they recognized that their lifestyle did not match their values. But in doing so, they created margin to discover passions they didn't even know they had.

YOUR PURPOSE, YOUR CHOICES

I said in chapter 1 that the ultimate benefit of minimalism is that it enables you to fulfill your greatest passions. But now we see that there's more, because minimalism can actually reveal, or at least clarify, what those passions are.

Take the plunge and get started. Let minimalism clarify your goals and values, and let your goals and values shape your personal expression of minimalism.

The goal of minimalism, let's remember, is not just to own less stuff. The goal of minimalism is to unburden our lives so we can accomplish more.

In the end, your particular practice of minimalism is going to look different from that of everyone else because your life is different from that of everyone else. You may have a large family, a small family, or no family. You may live on a farm, in a house, or in a studio apartment. You love music, movies, sports, or books. You practice art, or maybe you don't. Maybe you believe you were put on this earth to host beautiful dinner parties or offer your home as a place of respite and retreat for others.

Follow your passions to the best of your ability with the resources you possess. Fulfill your purpose with great focus by removing the distractions keeping you from it. And find a style of minimalism that works for you, one that is not cumbersome but freeing.

Be aware that your individual definition of minimalism will not emerge overnight. It will take you time to discover it. It will evolve, even change dramatically, as your life changes. It will require give-and-take. You will make some mistakes along the way. Because of that, your journey to minimalism will also require humility.

But ultimately you will remove the unneeded things from your life. And when you do, you will find more space for the things that really matter.

WHERE TO START MAKING IT YOUR OWN

Mark Twain has been credited as saying, "The two most important days in your life are the day you are born and the day you find out why." And I might add a third: the day you throw off any distraction and decide to pursue your purpose fully.

When you've individualized your approach to simplifying your life, it's easier to accomplish. It's more comfortable to you. You are more likely to sustain it. And it frees you up to express yourself and become who you were meant to be.

How, exactly, do you accomplish this?

If you want to clarify your own life goals, my advice is to start by examining yourself. Get a strong grip on your talents, abilities, and weaknesses and on the issues that get your blood boiling. To facilitate this, grab a sheet of paper and write out your answers to these questions:

1. What experiences, both good and bad, have shaped your life?
2. What similarities can you recognize in your most notable achievements?
3. What problems in the world are you most passionate about solving?
4. If money were not an issue, what line of work would you be most drawn to?
5. Which dreams in your life do you feel the most regret for not pursuing harder?

6. What is the lasting legacy you want to leave?
7. Whom do you most admire in life? What specific characteristics of this person do you want to emulate?

Continue to define your passions as you read this book. The theme of the big dream for your life will become increasingly important in the chapters that follow, culminating in the final chapter.

But for now, begin by recognizing that you were not born to live someone else's life. You were born to live yours. So determine today to be the best possible version of yourself through defining the approach to minimalism that works best for you.

I'm going to give you practical suggestions on ways to carry out your own approach to minimalism, starting with chapter 6. Before that, though, we need to be honest about the pressures we have to fight against: the external "pull" of consumeristic propaganda (chapter 4) and the internal "push" of materialistic greed (chapter 5).

The Fog of Consumerism

For my son's fifth birthday, he received a gift certificate to a popular toy retailer in town.

"What do you want from the toy store, Salem?" I asked him.

Without hesitation, Salem answered, "A skateboard."

I knew he wanted a skateboard for a while, and now he had enough resources to get one, so we hopped in the car and headed to the store. I was picturing the errand as being a quick one: pick out a skateboard, find a register to pay for it, drive home. This, however, was not to be the case.

As we entered the store, Salem was immediately transported to a different world. He seemed mesmerized by the colors and shapes and possibilities of the vast number of objects on the shelves. He wanted to look at and touch everything: the superhero figures, the Legos, the flashy electronics, and all the rest.

I grabbed his hand and steered him toward the skateboards. Unfortunately, as we made our way through the aisles, we came across a display dedicated to dinosaur-themed toys. I knew this was going to be a problem because at the time Salem had that inexplicable fascination with extinct reptiles that all kids his age seem to go through.

He stopped in front of a pop-up tent designed to look like a cave.

The packaging showed a young boy smiling from ear to ear as he played with toy dinosaurs around the tent.

Solemnly, Salem said to me, "Dad, I need this tent."

"But you have been saving money for months to buy a skateboard," I reminded him. "Besides, you would hardly ever play with this tent—the dinosaurs are not even included."

For some time we went back and forth, him with reasons why this tent was essential to his happiness, me with reasons why buying the tent would be a mistake.

Eventually I put my foot down. "Salem, we are not buying a dinosaur pop-up tent. That's final."

He was nearly in tears as I dragged him away from the dinosaur display. But a little later, when we walked out of the store with a skateboard as originally planned, he was smiling. He would go on to ride that skateboard countless times over the coming years.

As I've thought about that shopping experience in the years since, I've realized how much all of us are like five-year-olds when it comes to buying and owning things. We're captivated by the glamour of goods for sale, regardless of whether we need them or would enjoy them for long if we had them.

One reason this is the case is because we are each a part of a consumption-oriented culture. Consumerism surrounds us like the air we breathe, and like air, it's invisible. We hardly even know how much we are influenced by the philosophy that we must buy, buy, buy if we are to be happy. As we'll find out in the next chapter, our inner desires align with this external messaging, and as a result, consumerism feels normal and natural to us. We go along with the carnival of consumerism, only occasionally feeling a twinge of doubt about whether something might be wrong with it all.

The key to overcoming our consumeristic tendencies is to deliberately peer into our blind spot and see what we have been ignoring. We have to measure the magnitude of consumeristic propaganda and observe how thoroughly it permeates public discourse and our own personal outlook. We must also admit we have been influenced by it. For only then can we take a stand against consumerism's effects on our lives.

I should warn you, recognizing and rejecting consumerism is not easy. But the reward is well worth the effort. Pulling back the veil on consumerism's lies enables us to find more reliable sources of happiness.

HOW CONSUMERISM BECAME CONFUSED WITH HAPPINESS

The tendency toward greed and acquisitiveness has always been a human weakness. But consumerism as we know it today is a relatively modern phenomenon, dating back only about a century. As I will typically do in this book, I'll use my own country of the United States as an example. Similar stories could be told about other developed nations.

In the 1920s, when America had its first wave of affluence spreading to large swaths of the population, advertisers deliberately began to link ownership with happiness in the public mind. The advertisers got help in this endeavor from experts in the field of psychology. Ernest Dichter, a Freudian psychoanalyst who assisted advertisers, said, "To some extent, the needs and wants of people have to be continuously stirred up." [1]

The same strategy is still in operation. As one article explains,

> Today, an iPad, the right vacation, or the latest sneakers have become prerequisites for getting respect. Certain brands of beer are synonymous with friendship and a sense of community. An oversized house points to status and proof of your earnings and ability to provide for a family. These are all, of course, ideas created by advertisers whose clients profit when we buy more than we need. [2]

Advertisers have been so successful at playing on our selfish desires for ownership that today *buying* and *being happy* are considered virtually synonymous. It's as if the purpose of life is self-gratification and buying things is the only way to get there. We don't think about this—we just assume it.

Consider with me how pervasive this perspective really is. Our streets are lined with strip malls and retail stores. We measure our national well-being in gross domestic product, trade deficits, consumer confidence, and the rate of inflation. Every corner of our nation has been commercialized, even our national parks. We select our political leaders almost solely on what they promise to do for the health of the economy. The American Dream has been defined in dollar signs and square footage.

To make resisting consumerism even harder, some of the finest minds in our generation use every tool they can devise to craft us into even greedier consumers. Purchasing new things has never been easier—as simple as clicking a single button.

Now today, with increased opportunity for personal-data collection via technology, target marketing has allowed sellers to become even more effective. No longer do they know just our age, gender, and marital status. Today, corporations know our net worth, our personal preferences, our shopping habits, and our favorite books and movies. They know where we spend, when we spend, and how we spend. They have recorded every piece of data that could possibly be collected from our smartphones or our Internet browsers' history. And they use it every day to exploit our weaknesses.

In a sense, marketers know us better than we know ourselves. They feed on our insecurities and feelings of inadequacy. Society hijacks our passion and directs it toward material things. But nobody gets to the end of life wishing they had bought more things.

Why is that? *Because consumption never fully delivers on its promise of fulfillment or happiness.* Instead, it steals our freedom and results only in an unquenchable desire for more. It brings burden and regret. It distracts us from the very things that do bring us joy.

Now, resisting consumerism won't give us happiness in itself. An absence is just a nothingness. What matters is what we fill the empty space with. But we have to start somewhere. Resisting consumerism can keep us from being deceived and can give us the possibility of finding real happiness, whatever that might look like for each of us.

In the rest of this chapter, I want to highlight three areas of life where you can open your eyes to consumerism, spotting its effects where you might not have seen them before and exposing its true nature:

- the attitudes toward material ownership that you may
  have because of the generation you belong to,
- how the world has taught you to define success, and
- how marketers are trying to manipulate you when you
  shop.

NOTICE HOW YOUR GENERATION AFFECTS YOU

Chinese artist Song Dong's display titled *Waste Not* is a collection of household items owned by his late mother. The installation includes her entire inventory of physical possessions: cups, pots, basins, toothpaste tubes, shirts, buttons, ballpoint pens, bottle caps, bags, tubs, pieces of string, neckties, rice bowls, handbags, skipping ropes, stuffed animals, and dolls—ten thousand items in all. Every piece of it had been crammed into her Beijing home that was only a few hundred square feet in size. (The house is so small that it travels with the exhibit.)[3]

When I walked through the exhibit several years ago at the Museum of Modern Art in New York City, I felt a series of evolving emotions.

First, my emotional response was bewilderment. Why would anybody keep twelve empty tubes of toothpaste or hundreds of tiny pieces of string?

Second, amazement. How did all this stuff fit in that small house?

Third, disgust. What an awful way to live! Look at all that stuff in one home.

But finally—believe it or not—I wound up feeling gratitude.

You see, I began to understand that the exhibit illustrates not hoarding but the philosophy of an entire generation of people growing up in China during intense periods of war, rationing, starvation, expulsion, and constant shortages of goods. For Song Dong's mother, holding on to any and every worldly good felt as if it were a prerequisite for survival. What seemed to me like pathological hoarding was actually a rational response to external turmoil.

I have not had to live through the global and economic insecurity and upheaval that Song Dong's mother did. And consequently I don't feel like I need to hold on to everything that comes into my possession simply as preparation for famine or raiding rebels. I am free to choose to live with less. For that I am grateful.

Today, I still think of Song Dong's display whenever I observe how people of different eras and living conditions relate to material possessions. Because for each of us, when we were born, what stage of life we are in today, and what we have lived through and are still living through help to shape our relationship to things.

What does your generation say about your particular style of consumerism? You'll find it helpful to pay attention to this.

Generational analysis is not an exact science, by any means. Yet it can give some broad insights that aid in self-understanding.[4] Identify your generation, then begin to think through how it has influenced your attitudes toward accumulation and consumption.

- If you were born between 1928 and 1945, you are a part of the Silent Generation.
- If you were born between 1946 and 1964, you are a part of the Baby Boomer Generation.

- If you were born between 1965 and 1980, you are a part of Generation X.
- If you were born between 1981 and 2000, you are a part of the Millennial Generation.

Consumerism and the Silent Generation

The Silent Generation grew up during the Great Depression and World War II. Their generational views of possessions were shaped by a "waste not, want not" philosophy similar to that displayed by Song Dong's mother.

Members of this cohort grew up purchasing items that were built to last. They spent their growing-up years in an America with high unemployment and drought, followed by rationing during one of the harshest wars this world has ever seen. They lived frugally because they had to. And if they could save items, they did.

Today the survivors of the Silent Generation have reached their seventies and eighties. They are beginning to move into smaller living quarters—sometimes by choice, sometimes by necessity. But almost always with a heavy heart.

This helps us understand the growth of organizations such as the National Association of Senior Move Managers. Downsizing is difficult, painful work, both physically and emotionally. Even more so when you have lived in the same home for decades.

If you are a member of this generation, you may be facing the need to downsize. Minimizing is not just an advantage but a necessity for you. Now more than ever, it's important for you to ignore the consumerist appeal to buy more. Remember the lessons of simple living from your youth, and resist the prevailing attitude toward ownership. A life unburdened by excess possessions will make your remaining years more peaceful and more rewarding.

Consumerism and the Baby Boomer Generation

The Baby Boomer Generation, born immediately after World War II, grew up in a very different world from that of the Silents.

Following the end of World War II, America faced a severe housing shortage due to servicemen and women returning from war as well as unusually high birth rates. This gave rise to a sudden expansion of home building on the outskirts of cities. As a result, the Baby Boomers became the first generation raised in large numbers in the suburbs, with all the cultural forces that accompanied this way of life.

This generation benefited from an era of prosperity. During the Boomers' lifetimes, women began working outside the home in record numbers. Families became dual income for the first time in American history. Discretionary income reached a new high. And postwar optimism inspired stability and opportunity. Boomers became consumers of the first order.

The Baby Boomers' children are now grown, established, and on their own. And Boomers have reached, or are soon to reach, retirement age in record numbers. Many are choosing to downsize in hopes of making their resources last as they live the retirement lifestyle they have dreamed of, and worked hard for, for years. Minimalism may not come naturally to them, but they are beginning to see its benefits.

If you are a Boomer, you are probably questioning the equation that buying = happiness. Although you may have enjoyed a large house in the suburbs with the accompanying comforts of life in the past, perhaps now you are thinking more about the value of experiences over possessions. Maybe you are more focused on leaving a legacy than adding to a pile of possessions. If so, let me assure you that you're thinking in the right direction.

The generation that has brought about change in so many areas of society is capable of one more: changing its own perspective on ownership and consumption.

Consumerism and Generation X

My peers, Gen X, have been labeled cynical, individualistic, and self-absorbed survivalists. In many ways, we have been caught between American consumerism at its most unbridled and the dawning realities of what having too much really means, and we are maneuvering our way between these forces.

The phrase *latchkey kid* was coined to define our childhood. We grew up in families of working parents with disposable income but often seemingly with little time and energy for their children. Our parents purchased homes in the suburbs but sometimes at the expense of family dinners around the table.

Generation X came of age during the technological revolution. Most of us began kindergarten with no computers in our schools but learned typing on a word processor, then graduated college by e-mailing papers to our professors. Because of the tech revolution, our world has become increasingly mobile. Due to our individualistic pursuits and distrust of institutions, our generation will average seven career changes during our lifetimes, something unimagined by our grandparents.

But kids have a way of changing people. And Generation Xers, now in middle age, are parenting children of all ages. Most Gen Xers are responding to the parental examples they grew up with by embracing the opposite paradigm: "latchkey kids" have become "helicopter parents." And with Baby Boomer grandparents who are used to showing love by buying gifts, Gen X homes are quickly becoming overrun with clutter.

If you are a Gen Xer, your days of peak earning may be immediately in front of you. The "advantages" that consumerism is holding out to you may seem more within your reach than ever before. Don't be fooled. You know how overaccumulation has already begun to affect you for the worse. Say no to consumerism now, before it's too late.

Consumerism and the Millennial Generation

In some ways, minimalism is a natural way of life for the Millennial Generation.

The Millennials are the first generation born after the technological revolution (though there are no signs of its slowing down). Their world is smaller, and they expect to be connected to technology and one another at all times. Coffee shops have become the new offices, collaboration has become the new competition, and mobility has become the new stability. As many Millennials will tell you, it is difficult to live a mobile lifestyle with a house full of stuff.

This generation is the most environmentally conscious of all age groups, and this influences their buying habits significantly.

Technological connectedness has brought new opportunities for the "sharing economy" in which assets (bikes, cars, housing) are not owned by individuals but shared communally. Access has replaced ownership.

Additionally, the Internet has established a worldwide flea market. When nearly every product available to humankind can arrive at my doorstep in less than twenty-four hours with just the click of a button, I have less need to stockpile an inventory of items in my house.

Minimalism is attractive to the Millennials. Current design trends embody this movement. Technology has made it easier than ever to own less. And the minimalist lifestyle aligns with many of their deeply rooted generational values.[5]

It is important to note, however, that this generation has graduated college and entered the workforce in the middle of the Great Recession. Underemployment, coupled with record levels of student debt, have left some Millennials with little discretionary income even if they wanted to be consumeristic. It remains to be seen whether the economic conditions of their upbringing have shaped them to be minimal by nature or whether future economic growth will cause them to slip into the same excesses of ownership that previous generations have fallen for. For the Millennials' sake, I hope the former holds true.

If you are a Millennial, why not lead the way to a new minimalist paradigm that can free us all? You're better positioned to do it than anybody else.

It is helpful for each of us to understand how our generational cohort nuances our relationship to the consumer culture. It's also helpful to recognize a dangerous attitude that seemingly all generations in America are prone to: confusing excess with success.

OPEN YOUR EYES TO WHAT YOU'RE PRAISING

Our world applauds success. And well it should. It is entirely appropriate to champion those who develop their talents, work hard, and overcome obstacles.

Unfortunately, however, our society is also fixated on praising excess. We are not the first people to worship conspicuous consumption, but we have taken the practice to new heights (or rather, lows). Magazines overexpose the details of the lives of the rich and famous. News publications rank people according to their net worth. Reality television applauds the lifestyles of those who live in luxury. The Internet attracts readers with countless stories about those who appear to be living the good life.

In our own lives we do the same. We comment on the size of the houses in the neighborhood nearby. We point out the luxury car in the lane next to us. We envy fashionable clothes and designer handbags. We make jokes about marrying into money. We dream of a life without limits because of our riches.

We desire to live the life of those who seem to have it all. In our hearts and in our affections, we praise those who live with excess.

But we are making a big mistake.

Success and *excess* are not the same.

Possession of riches is often arbitrary. Sometimes people achieve financial gain through hard work and dedication. But not always.

Sometimes financial wealth is a result of heritage, dishonesty, or just plain luck. In those cases, the rich have earned no praise for their wealth.

Besides, regardless of how the wealthy have come by their riches, purchasing excess is rarely the wisest use of money. Just because we have the financial resources to afford something does not mean it is the best option for us. So why do we keep celebrating those who use money selfishly?

Our world checks the wrong scoreboard. Those who live in excess are not necessarily the ones who have the most fulfilled lives. Often it is those who live quietly, modestly, and contentedly with a simple life who are the happiest. Those are the choices we should be celebrating and the lives we should be emulating. Yet this definition of success is foreign to most of us.

How are you making material excess out to be something it is not? What does it reveal about the hold that consumerism has on your heart and mind?

Admire success. But do not celebrate excess. Learning to know the difference will change your life.

So will wising up to the strategies implemented with the sole purpose of convincing you to buy more than you need.

SPOT THE TOOLS OF THE TRADE

We love to shop. For proof, look no further than Black Friday.

In America, Thanksgiving—a holiday previously dedicated to giving thanks for what we have—has become a day for families to begin their biggest shopping spree of the year. More than 140 million Americans expect to go shopping on the weekend of Black Friday. During the holiday season alone, Americans spend over $600 billion.[6]

Marketers and advertising agencies have obviously succeeded at their jobs. In 2013, US marketers spent $171 billion on media advertising (digital, magazines, newspapers, billboards, radio, TV) throughout the year.[7]

If you think you are immune (or too smart) to be influenced by the power of advertisements, you are wrong. Corporations do not spend $171 billion in advertising *hoping* to influence you; they spend $171 billion in advertising because they *know* they will influence you.

Of course, they don't want you to know that. In fact, the more you believe you are not influenced by advertisements, the better they have done their job. None of us like to think we can be easily influenced by a stranger with a hidden agenda. For that reason, most successful ad campaigns seek to make an impression on us by creating a positive connection with our subconscious. They subtly promise that our sex lives will improve because of their cologne, our parties will be livelier with their soda, our reputations will improve because of their cars, and we will feel safer because of their insurance.

They accomplish this in any number of ways: the color of their logo, the placement of their product on the screen, the celebrity endorsement, even the direction of photographed eye glances and pupil sizes.

But the marketers' tools of the trade that separate us from our money go far beyond commercials and jingles. Media marketing is an art, but it is more than that. Campaigns to influence our spending are also rooted in science and an intimate understanding of how to manipulate our minds.

Here are some of the most common marketing ploys in the world of retail today. They are so commonplace that you will recognize almost all of them. As you do, keep in mind that each method is specifically designed and utilized to convince you to buy, buy, and buy some more.

- *Loyalty points and cards.* Merchants offer us free rewards when we spend a certain amount of money at their stores. They often prompt us to shop or buy things we don't need, just for the satisfaction of redeeming the reward.

- *Retail-store credit cards.* These cards offer us a percentage discount on our purchase if we sign up today. This works out well for the issuers: research shows you will spend up to twice as much with that card in hand.[8] And they will have collected all your personal data and shopping habits too.

- *Scarcity mind-set.* Marketers routinely fabricate a sense of urgency to compel us to purchase. Item on sale for a limited time! Package deal will soon be gone! Limited number of seats remaining! Each of these claims forces us to make a snap decision. Usually, we end up making the wrong one.

- *Instant markdown.* The CEO of JCPenney was fired because he decided to remove sale prices from items in their stores. His strategy was to mark every item as low as it could be priced all the time—no hassles or sales, just low-priced items. Unfortunately, the strategy failed as sales plummeted. Lowering the original prices resulted in lower sales. How could this be? Eventually, researchers determined that consumers were more likely to purchase an item marked "on sale" than they were to buy the exact same product at the same price without a "sale" sticker on it. They went on to conjecture that most consumers have no idea how much a product should cost in the first place. By artificially inflating the original price of an item, retailers are able to trick consumers into thinking they are getting a deal on the item at the sale price, even if they aren't.[9]

- *Decoy pricing.* Restaurants will often price one or two items on the menu unreasonably high even though they know few people will purchase the item. By setting one price at the top of the range, they make everything else look cheaper. In retail, this is accomplished by pricing one item significantly higher than similar items next to it (large-screen televisions, for example).
- *Loss leader.* A common trick among grocery stores (though they are not alone in this) is to offer one item at a discounted price just to get you in the door. Even though they take a small loss on the sale-priced item, they are confident you will walk out of the store having purchased more than that one thing.

- *Samples.* For shoppers, free food samples represent a fun
  opportunity to snack or test out a featured item the store
  hopes we will enjoy and purchase. But for the store, there
  is more strategy behind it. Whenever we eat a sample, we
  tell our body that it is time to eat, and our brains begin
  searching for food. Some studies report that 40 percent of
  people who accept an in-store sample will eventually buy
  a food item, even though they hadn't planned on buying
  it.[10] Just because you passed up buying the featured item
  doesn't mean the store didn't manipulate you into
  spending money.

- *Architectural layouts.* Most of us know grocery stores
  place the staples of produce, dairy, meat, and baked goods
  in opposite corners so we have to walk the length of the
  store, providing more time for them to capture our
  attention. But did you know shopping malls are purposefully built in a way to disorient the shopper to encourage
  browsing and impulse purchases? Or that outlet malls are
  purposefully built on the outskirts of major cities to
  encourage shoppers to stay longer and spend more because
  they made a "special trip" to be there? Almost every retail
  building reflects a specific design strategy for bringing out
  our consumeristic tendencies.

These represent only a few of the ways marketers try to compel us
to buy more than we need. Just consider the lengths that retail stores
(and other industries) will go to in order to fool you into buying. This
fierce battle is being waged against us every single day. Begin to

recognize these commonly used devices so you can more quickly notice the effects they have on you.

Additionally, it is important for you to recognize your individual weaknesses and trigger points. Do certain stores tempt you to make unnecessary purchases? Are there products, addictions, or pricing patterns (such as clearance sales) that prompt an almost automatic response from you? Maybe when you're feeling specific emotions—sadness, loneliness, grief, or stress—you're more likely to engage in mindless consumption.

Consumerism is pervasive in our culture. We have to train our eyes to see it in operation. Because then we can resist its destructive allure.

A BEAUTIFUL LIBERATION

Journalist Margot Starbuck interviewed me over the phone for an article on the topics of consumption, parenting, holiday gift giving, and generosity. The phone conversation lasted about forty-five minutes, and when it was over, I thought that would be the end of our connection.

Little did I know the effect this conversation would have on the other end of the line.

Just days after our conversation, I received an e-mail from Margot. I was expecting a follow-up question or request for a clarification. Instead, she began sharing with me how her view of possessions had begun to change after our short conversation.

She wrote, "Joshua, I really enjoyed chatting last week. Since we

spoke, I got rid of one thousand things (scary how easy it was!)."
With the help of her teenage children, Margot had wandered through
their home in Durham, North Carolina, removing anything they
no longer needed. Soon they had donated numerous bags and boxes
of household items to local charities—over a thousand things in just
a handful of days!

I loved hearing this, and I asked Margot to keep me informed
about any further adventures in minimalism.

Three months after our initial conversation, Margot e-mailed me
again. This time, she wrote to me directly from The Streets of South-
point Mall in Durham. She had arrived early for a lunch appointment
and found herself wandering through the familiar halls. But on this
occasion, having become a convert to owning less, she saw in a new light
all the items that used to capture her attention: jewelry at Claire's, boots
at Nordstrom, and white denim jackets at Sears. Her e-mail read like
this: "Joshua, for maybe the first time ever, I walked through a mall not
wanting anything. Instead, I experienced perfect satisfaction knowing I
already have more than enough. It feels like a beautiful liberation."

Liberation from the need to possess. And liberation from con-
forming to a society built on consumerism. This is the promise of
minimalism: to rejoice at the sight of all the things we do not need.
And to have our lives finally freed to pursue the things we want to do.
I want you to have the same joy, to experience the same liberation.

Achieving this liberation will require each of us to recognize and
resist the consumeristic society in which we live. It will also require us
to peer inward, to identify the vulnerabilities in our own natures.

The Want Within

Sitting in their living room early one evening, Anthony and Amy Ongaro were growing increasingly frustrated as they discussed their finances. They had been invited to go on a trip with some family members, and they really wanted to do it, but these types of opportunities always seemed slightly too expensive to pull off. There just wasn't quite enough money in their bank account.

"How come, whenever we have a chance to do something that would cost more than a few hundred bucks, it's out of reach? I don't get it," said Amy.

"I know," agreed Anthony. "It's not like we don't both have good jobs. Money's coming in. So where does it all go?"

Just then the doorbell rang. Anthony went to answer it, getting to the door just in time to see the back of a delivery person disappearing into a brown van. An Amazon package lay on the doorstep.

Anthony's eyes lit up. This must be the indestructible cell-phone case he had ordered. Or maybe it was the portable charger he had been waiting for.

Beaming with excitement, he opened the package in front of Amy. Sure enough, the cell-phone case.

Absorbed in checking out his new purchase, Anthony didn't notice that Amy grew silent and sat without moving. She was thinking. In her mind she had made a connection. Finally she said to Anthony, "Maybe this is the reason we can't go on vacation."

"What? This phone accessory? Honey, it only cost thirty-five bucks."

"Not just this, but this and everything else you order online."

"I do like to click and buy," Anthony admitted.

After making some tea, the pair went online and pulled up their Amazon ordering history for the last four years. The results shocked them. They had spent more than $10,000 over that period of time, nearly all of it on items under $40 each. These were products of no real significance to the couple. Anthony and Amy couldn't even remember many of them.

Staring at their ordering history in disbelief was the beginning of greater self-understanding for the Ongaros. One major reason this childless couple with two incomes couldn't afford things that would really have meant something to them was because they had been frittering away their money. Every few days they were making small online purchases. Each time, it gave them a dopamine rush that made them feel good for a little while. Now, however, they could see that the collective damage was devastating.

Each of us needs to seek the same kind of self-understanding. If we want to get more out of less, we need to look inward and examine our motives for the buying decisions we make.

We saw in the previous chapter how marketers and the culture in general influence our shopping and consumption habits. Society's pressure is indeed great. But we will fall short in our analysis if we place all the blame on external forces. A lot of the blame (I'm sorry I have to point this out) falls on *us*. Nobody is forcing us to buy their products. *We* decide to overspend and overaccumulate.

Can you agree?

For you, the reasons for buying too much could be many. Like the Ongaros, you might be buying things for the short-term rush it gives you. In this chapter we'll be looking at some other motivations you might have; you may be buying things in an attempt to fulfill a basic human need such as security, acceptance, or contentment.

But what I argue is that all these motivations really have the same fatal flaw: you're looking to material possessions to provide what you can only get somewhere else. No wonder you feel cheated and disappointed!

I'll give you this promise: Once you get to the *why* of your un-necessary purchases—the hidden motivations causing you to buy— then possessions will begin to lose their power over you. You'll be able to find real happiness and pursue significance in your life through minimalism. But first, as counselors like to say, you've got some inner work to do, my friend.

MINIMALISM HOLDS THE MIRROR

Back in chapter 3, I explained that beginning to pursue minimalism can help to reveal or clarify your goals for your life. A similar heu-ristical process plays out with regard to our inner motivations. As we begin to get rid of things we don't want, it forces moments of self-discovery and requires us to stand face-to-face with some of our hidden motivations.

When my wife and I began going through our home and removing possessions, we dropped off many piles of things at Goodwill and other local charities. Taking the first minivan load of things to the charities felt great. So did the second and third. We felt freer and lighter with each trip, and I'm going to talk more about the value of donation in a later chapter.

But by about the fourth minivan load of unneeded things we dropped off at a collection center, we started to ask ourselves some difficult questions. Namely, "Why in the world did we own four minivan loads' worth of things we didn't need? Why did we buy all this excess in the first place? What were we thinking?"

Eventually I began to say to myself, *Well, maybe I am more in love with stuff than I ever realized. Maybe I am more susceptible to the world's messaging than I thought. Maybe I am trying to find happiness in the things that I own despite repeatedly saying I'm not. Maybe there are a lot of lies I have begun to believe.*

These were difficult answers to difficult questions. Nobody enjoys discovering such things about oneself. But they came from a realization that I could never have had until I had started giving away my things.

And that is why minimalism is important to our self-discovery. As we remove the clutter from our homes, we learn more about ourselves, and we lay the foundation for greater pursuits, however we decide to define them for ourselves.

Let your journey toward minimalism and your own thoughtful

self-evaluation reveal to you your inner motivations regarding security. It is one of three areas of basic human need that, when pursued in the wrong way, contribute to an overaccumulation of goods.

SURRENDERING THE GOLDEN FORTRESS

Ask yourself, *Am I buying too much stuff because deep down I think it will insulate me from the harms of a chancy world? And if so, what is that costing me?*

In our society, too many of us believe security can be adequately found in the personal ownership of possessions. Of course there is a grain of truth in that belief. Certainly, food and water, clothing and shelter are essential for survival. But the list of possessions that we truly need for life is quite short, and most of us already have those things.

The reality is, we have too quickly confused needs with wants and security with comfort. As a result, many of us collect large stockpiles of possessions in the name of security when we are actually accumulating comfort (or desired pleasure). We work long hours to purchase these things. And we construct bigger and bigger houses to store them.

We dream of a future that includes larger paychecks and sizable savings accounts. We plot and plan to acquire them because we think they provide lasting security. If that costs us in other areas of life, such as our family and friendships, then that's the way it goes. The source of security seems so important that we can't give up our pursuit of more.

One day I received an e-mail that was gut-wrenching to me. A woman wrote,

> I'm a working mom of three young boys. I ran across your website while researching ways in which people have made a one-income household work for a family of five.
>
> My husband and I have worked our tails off over the last fifteen years to advance in our careers. In doing so, we have accumulated a lot of material possessions. We didn't start out materialistic, really. Over the years, though, we have engorged our lifestyle, including a large home and even a modest lake retreat.
>
> Two weeks ago we overheard my eight-year-old son tell a friend, "Mommy and Daddy aren't home a lot. We don't see them very much."
>
> My husband and I stopped dead in our tracks. Our hearts broke. Is all of our stuff really worth it? Of course not.
>
> We are trying to figure out the "how." We are looking over our budget, trying to find a renter for our log cabin by the lake, and working to have my husband quit his job to be a stay-at-home dad. I am wondering if you have any pointers to help us along this path.

This woman and her husband felt that they *needed* to work. They felt that they *needed* more money and more things. They believed that their family wouldn't be safe and secure and well provided for without the fruits of many long days on the job . . . until they realized that they were providing something very different from what their family really needed.

EMBRACING SECURITY

Our lives are fragile and this world is unpredictable. It's no wonder why we all long for security.

Yet lasting security can never be found in temporal possessions. The contingencies of life are too many, and the power of possessions to protect us is too weak. This is why we always desire more. We never arrive at a full sense of security.

So what should we do, given our legitimate need for a sense of security?

We should look to the very things we so often sacrifice in our pursuit of more and more possessions: relationships.

Margaret Clark, a professor of psychology at Yale, says that a sense of security can come from both material goods and from supportive relationships. But it's easy to get out of balance. Clark writes,

> Humans are social creatures with vulnerabilities. Close
> relationships afford protections. For examples, infants
> wouldn't survive without other people. But material posses-
> sions also afford protection and security. Humans need food,
> clothing and shelter to survive. So, it takes a mix of things to
> make you feel secure. But, if you heighten one source of
> security, people feel less concerned about the others.[1]

Dr. Clark bases this finding on two research projects she and her colleagues conducted. The researchers concluded that those who do not feel internally secure in their personal relationships will often put a higher value on physical possessions.

I would suggest that the opposite is often true as well: those who are overestimating what their possessions can do for them tend to undervalue and put too little work into their relationships.

If you decide that one of your motives for overaccumulating is because you're relying on your things to give you a sense of safety, then I urge you to cut back on buying and owning and instead put more effort into how you relate to the people around you. Rich relationships with your family and friends can not only give you joy but also make you feel safe in a web of caring. At the same time you will be contributing to others' sense of security and satisfaction too—so much more productive than building your own private fortress of wealth!

So stop trusting too much in money and material possessions as your source of security. They will never deliver it. Minimize your ownership, and you'll be freed up to find real security.

That's one motivation that might be influencing our overaccumulation. Another one is a desire for social acceptance.

WHEN THE "RIGHT" STUFF IS THE WRONG STUFF

Kim and I were pretty sure our kids needed glasses. Both Salem and Alexa had begun to squint when reading digital clocks or fine print. So we recently took them to an ophthalmologist, who confirmed our suspicions and prescribed eyeglasses.

What is interesting is how our kids have reacted to their new eyewear.

Alexa, our grade-school-age daughter, picked purple frames and kind of likes wearing her glasses. It certainly helps that her friends refer to them as "adorable."

But our son, Salem, who has recently become a teenager? How does he feel about wearing his glasses?

Well, when he is home alone with us, he doesn't find wearing glasses to be a problem. He can see the computer screen better, he can read books more easily, and he can read the clock on the oven without having to stand up and walk closer. But when he is with his friends, he hates wearing his glasses and does so only when absolutely necessary. His glasses cause him embarrassment around his friends.

Ah, some things never change. I can remember being embarrassed in exactly the same way when I was Salem's age.

I wish I could say that only the young are susceptible to embarrassment. But the truth is, even as we get older, we continue to feel embarrassed or to fear being put in a position where we might become embarrassed. The only difference is that the causes of our embarrassment change. In many cases, we feel embarrassed because we don't have what other adults have or we don't have expensive-enough things. It's not just about glasses now. It's about cars, homes, vacations, and so many more of the things that adults buy or wish they could buy.

What I want to point out is that these feelings of embarrassment stem from our baseline understanding of normal. Nobody feels embarrassed for just being normal. It's when we deviate from the norm that we might become embarrassed. Yet our understanding of normal is entirely subjective, based on the measurement most often defined by the social groups with which we surround ourselves. Consider clothing.

I would venture to guess that you and most of your friends wear similar clothing. Not that you all have the same taste in fashion, but generally speaking, both the quantity and the quality of your wardrobes are much the same. You shop at many of the same stores. Your closets are similarly sized. The dollar amounts you spend on any one outfit probably don't vary too greatly.

Why is this?

It's because most of us choose to spend our personal time with people who are similar to us. We feel comfortable and accepted among them.

But when you are pulled from your regular social circle, you may begin to feel self-conscious about things you wouldn't normally think twice about.

Imagine attending a party or work function with people from a higher socioeconomic class than your own. These people arrive wearing fancy dresses and tailored suits. Suddenly, the clothes you used to wear without any misgivings begin to seem inadequate to you. You notice that they are faded, worn, ill fitting, or less costly than the clothes others around you are wearing. And in this moment you begin to feel a twinge of embarrassment, not because the clothes are any different from what you normally wear, but because your immediate culture's expression of normal has changed dramatically.

That kind of reaction is typical. But it should make us realize how arbitrary our sense of "normal" is. And it should reveal to us that we're buying too many things because we hope that they will make others accept us and that they will help us feel comfortable and "normal."

Because we live in a culture that normalizes the pursuit of appearances, possessions, and selfish gain, feelings of awkwardness and shame arise within us when we do not measure up in these areas. We get embarrassed that our clothes are last year's fashion, that our vehicle costs less than our neighbor's, or that our house is smaller than our guest's. We apologize for the worn carpet, make excuses for the outdated kitchen, or explain why we haven't updated the countertops yet.

We are getting embarrassed over all the wrong things! Social norms and acceptance are not really what we should be embarrassed about.

What if, instead of being embarrassed over the brand of our clothing, we became embarrassed over the enormity of our walk-in closet?

What if, instead of being embarrassed over the type of car we drive, we became embarrassed over how often we take the luxury of automobile ownership for granted?

What if, instead of being embarrassed because our house seems too small, we became embarrassed over the amount of unused space within it?

What if, instead of being embarrassed over the quality and quantity of our possessions, we became embarrassed over how much money we have spent on our own selfish pursuits?

What if excess became the cause of embarrassment? And responsible living that championed generosity became the norm?

Maybe then we could become a little more proud of "normal."

Are you buying too many things and spending too much money because you want others to like and accept you? Change your view of what's acceptable and what's normal, and you will be freed from embarrassment and freed to make more of a positive difference in this world.

A Land Near at Hand

A desire for security and a craving for acceptance are two basic human objectives that we can foolishly try to fulfill by overaccumulating. But there is one more such need I want to highlight: contentment. We all want to feel like we've arrived. Like we've got all we want and are satisfied. We all want to reach the land called Contentment.

People look for contentment in all sorts of places. Some look for it in a high-paying job and yet are discontent the first time they are passed over for a raise. Some look for it in a large home and yet are discontent every time it needs improvements or maintenance. Many have sought contentment in a department store, believing one more item will finally fulfill them, yet when they get home with their purchase, they still feel like something is missing.

It's as if contentment is a destination that recedes into the distance every time we approach it. That's inevitable when our concept of contentment depends upon material abundance. Is it possible that we have been taught to look for contentment in all the wrong places?

What if contentment is actually found in the opposite place from where we have been looking? What if contentment is found not in accumulating things for ourselves but in meeting the needs of others?

It's true that the less we need, the more we can give away. But what if the inverse is also true? What if the more we give away, the less we need? In other words, what if generosity leads to contentment?

People who give away possessions hold their remaining possessions in higher esteem. People who give their time make better use of their remaining time. And people who donate money are less wasteful with the money left over.

When you begin helping others, sharing your money, possessions, and time (a topic we'll be exploring in depth in chapter 11), you will find yourself learning to be content. The practice will give you a finer appreciation for what you own, who you are, and what you have to offer.

Generous people have less desire for more. They find fulfillment, meaning, and value outside of the acquisition of possessions. They learn to find joy in what they already possess, and they give away the rest. They discover the secret to contentment. It's surprisingly close at hand.

So if a misguided search for contentment is motivating your pursuit of too much, my advice is that you take control of your attitude. Don't engage in when-and-then thinking: *When I get _____, then I will be happy.* Instead, remember that your happiness does not depend on your acquisition of any possession. Your happiness is based solely on your decision to be happy—and this may be one of the most important life lessons you can ever learn.

There were many reasons Kim and I chose to become minimalist and simplify our lives. We were frustrated with clutter. We were stuck in our finances. We discovered that we were wasting time managing our possessions. We realized we weren't finding joy there. And we determined that we value other things far more than our physical belongings.

As we began simplifying our home and removing unneeded possessions, generosity became a natural by-product: we needed to get rid of things, and we quickly found people who needed them.

As we did, we found donating to be far more rewarding than owning. Our view of material possessions and the excess that so many seek changed completely. We didn't want more stuff. We wanted to experience more of the abundance we found in giving.

Contentment took up residence in our home.

DO THE TWIST

Wanting to feel safe, wanting to feel normal around others, wanting to feel like we've arrived—all these motivations are natural. There's nothing wrong with any of them. But when we think that making lots of money and buying an overabundance of possessions will give us these results, we're almost always disappointed.

Security, acceptance, and contentment are not the only hidden motivations that might be driving you to buy too much. The more you remove, additional unhealthy motivations will begin to emerge. They may be difficult to uncover, but it is important that you do so. Some people buy more than they should because they have a sense of inadequacy and try to compensate for it with accumulation. Others are jealous of friends or acquaintances and are trying to keep up with them. And pretty much all of us are selfish.

In my experience, however, the desires for security, acceptance, and contentment are three nearly universal motivations.

We need to recognize what's inside us that's driving our purchasing decisions, because only then can we rob materialism of its power to distract us from what could bring us real happiness and meaning.

Again, it's not that things such as security, acceptance, and contentment are bad. It's just that material things have limited ability to satisfy those needs. That's why we need to put a twist on our natural motivations:

- Instead of seeking security in buying lots of stuff, seek it in loving relationships with other people.
- Instead of trying to earn acceptance from others by owning the same stuff they have, rewrite your definition of what success looks like to you.
- Instead of chasing contentment by always adding to your stuff, let contentment come to you by appreciating what you have and giving away what you don't need.

The war to take control of our motivations is never ending. Even if we have been pursuing minimalism for a while, materialism can still grab hold of our hearts.

Whenever it does, use it to uncover your hidden motivations, and redirect those motivations to find the happiness you really want, not the false happiness money and possessions promise.

And now you're ready to begin the actual process of minimizing!

It's about to get really practical. Your home is going to start look-ing different. Along the way, as unneeded possessions disappear, new possibilities for your life are going to emerge.

I'm going to teach you how to . . .

- start easy in minimizing your possessions (chapter 6)
- move on to tackle the harder areas of your home (chapter 7)
- use experiments to figure out how little you actually need (chapter 8)
- establish new habits to secure your gains permanently (chapter 9)

My advice is that while you're reading these upcoming chapters, you begin putting their principles into practice. Read a chapter; re-move some unneeded items from your home. Read another chapter; remove some more.

If you haven't already started minimizing your home and finding a better life because of it, now is the time.

Take It Easy

When I speak up for minimalism with people who are just starting to consider this way of life, I can almost see them trying to picture themselves getting rid of their stuff. Then the objections come out. They ask,

"What about my sentimental items and family heirlooms?"

"What about my books?"

"What about our kids' toys?"

"What do I do with all my craft supplies?"

"My husband will never go along with this idea. What should I do about his stuff?"

These questions are all different, and yet if we look closely, we can see that they have a point of similarity. And it is this similarity that causes too many people to get stuck in their journey toward a freer life *before they even begin.*

Consider the questions again. Each focuses on the apparently toughest thing to declutter in the person's home, whether heirlooms, books, toys, supplies, or a loved one's possessions. Each questioner's mind has raced to whatever seems the most difficult area in his or her home to minimize. That's understandable. But it shows me that each person is focusing on the obstacles, not the opportunities. And I think there's a better way.

My response to such questions is always the same: "You don't need to start with the hard stuff. Start easy. Start small. Just start somewhere."

This is my message for you too.

For now, don't worry about the toughest tasks in simplifying. Instead, begin your more-of-less journey at the easiest possible place. Build up momentum by clearing the clutter from your automobile, a drawer, your living room, or maybe your bathroom cupboard. You will begin to experience success and see the benefits of living with less. As you do, you will learn the skills necessary for confronting the more challenging areas in your home—and life.

In later chapters, we will dive into some of the deeper questions and address the areas of your life where it's harder to purge. I'll be providing answers to your questions and suggesting methods to help you move past your obstacles. But here I want to offer baby steps so you can begin taking back your life from your stuff. As I mentioned earlier, your definition and practice of minimalism is going to look different from mine or anyone else's. But there are some common methods we can all use to get started. You'll find them so easy to grasp, so easy to use, and so encouraging that you'll want to start today.

You've got this.

DECLARING YOUR WHY

First, let's review what minimalism is. It is the intentional promotion of the things we most value and the removal of anything that distracts us from them. Even though we're now talking about decluttering, the ultimate purpose is to put ourselves in a position where it's easier to fulfill our life's goals.

This leads me to the first baby step in your minimizing journey.

I encourage you, before you remove even one item from your home, to sit down and articulate one or more reasons why you want to minimize. Take time to think about this, if you have not already done so. The possibilities are endless—and will be entirely unique to you, your purpose, and your values.

I'm not saying that you have to have every last detail of your goals nailed down right now. As I said in chapter 3, your purposes will drive your simplifying, and your simplifying will refine your purposes. The one enhances the other in an ongoing discovery process. But as far as you know them now, define your reasons for de-owning and decluttering, and keep these reasons before you. Actually write them down. Here are some examples:

I want to get out of debt and start saving money for retirement.

I want a schedule that's less hectic.

I want to be available to help my parents as they grow older.

I want to climb mountains on every continent of the world.

I want to spend a year volunteering at a clinic in Haiti.

I want to downsize to a condo.

I want to be free to coach my child's sports team.

I want to stop teaching music lessons and join a chamber orchestra.

I want to spend my evenings with my family instead of straightening up the house.

I want to invite people over without worrying about what a mess my house is.

When you have written down your goal (or goals), post it in a place where you will see it often. It will serve as important motivation going forward. And there will be times when you desperately need the inspiration. Without it, you might forget why you're filling a box to take to Goodwill or you might lose interest in posting that china hutch on Craigslist.

Before any of us can minimize our homes and lives, we must be convinced the lifestyle is worth our effort. Your statement of purposes for simplifying will remind you of what you want out of the process you're starting. And it's so easy to do.

But that's just the beginning.

QUICK GRABS

After creating a list of your goals and turning to face your surroundings, where do you start in actually clearing out all that stuff you own?

It shouldn't be hard to find a place. Have you heard of the 80/20 rule? It's a generality, but it's proved true in many areas of life. As applied to our possessions, it means that we use 20 percent of our stuff 80 percent of the time, and we use the other 80 percent of our stuff only 20 percent of the time. So within that 80 percent of your stuff that mostly just lies around, there should be plenty of easy pickings when you start to minimize.

I recommend beginning in the areas of your home that you use frequently. Living rooms, bedrooms, and bathrooms, in particular, are great places to start. Typically, they are easier and take less time to declutter than kitchens, offices, or attics. But more importantly, because you use these rooms often, you will quickly experience the benefits of minimalism by making a difference in those areas. Removing clutter from your living room allows for a more peaceful, less distracted time of relaxation or family bonding. A minimized bathroom will make getting ready in the morning easier. A decluttered bedroom offers benefits both day and night. As you remove the excess from these places in your home, you will notice the positive effects almost immediately.

Remember, right now you're focused on choosing easy battles, scoring quick wins, and establishing momentum in your decluttering journey. Do the obvious tidying up in the areas where you spend most of your time. Most likely you can accomplish this first step in just a few hours. Don't make any hard decisions yet. Simply grab an empty bag, and remove everything you can easily part with, along with anything that you don't even *want* in your home anymore, items that you probably should have gotten rid of long ago. Just put them in the bag, and set them aside for now. You will sort them later.

This isn't a thorough cleaning. You haven't dealt with your whole house yet. But already you can step back, look at the result, and start feeling the peace that comes from living in a home that has enough but not too much.

Let me tell you the first space I cleaned out. It happened to be a space that I took with me on the go.

When Calm Descended on a Corolla

As I said in the first chapter, I was cleaning out my garage one Saturday when I was originally introduced to the idea of owning less. There's a sequel to the story.

That evening I climbed into our Toyota Corolla to drive it back into the garage. When I did, I noticed something I had never really paid attention to before: unneeded things everywhere. Sunglasses never worn. CDs never listened to. Maps never used. Rooting about, I found stuffed animals, Happy Meal toys, ketchup packets, stacks of napkins, and children's books in the backseat. The driver's door alone was littered with pens, receipts, and coins that had fallen into its storage compartment.

In many ways, this car was a microcosm of the life I had been living. Mess and excess everywhere. Only this mess was one I took with me wherever I went.

I took a deep breath. Then I decided (remember, after hearing about minimalism only hours earlier) that this would be as easy a project as any with which to get started. I grabbed a plastic bag and put into it everything that didn't absolutely need to stay in the car. I left only the title, the proof of insurance, and the car manual in the glove compartment. I took away everything else. Then I hauled the bag away for sorting later.

With that simple act of cleaning my car, our family's minimalist journey had officially begun. The whole project took fewer than fifteen minutes.

I began to enjoy the benefits almost immediately.

The following morning, a Sunday, I woke early. The church where I worked was ten miles from home, and arriving early on Sundays was habit for me. In the quiet of the morning, I dressed, ate, and headed for my car.

I vividly remember entering my now clutter-free vehicle. The physical space around me felt different from the way it had before. It was not just cleaner but also calmer—like a focused breath of fresh air. The car contained fewer items to distract me, and each of the remaining items was there for a good reason. As I drove, I could feel my mind relax, allowing me to focus on the day ahead.

I knew this feeling of calm and focus was one I wanted in all aspects of my life. I couldn't believe how easy and quick it had been to start experiencing the advantages to owning less stuff.

ROOM BY ROOM

After making an initial sweep to clear out your lived-in spaces (or in my case, my driven-in space), the next stage is to carry out a more thorough process of minimizing your possessions. Go room by room until you've tackled your whole house.

Now you'll start asking some of the harder questions: What,

realistically, needs to stay? And what can go? What possessions are adding value to my life? And what possessions are distracting from it?

Remember that you don't have to figure it all out at once or get the whole house done in a hurry. Focus on one specific area at a time: a room, a closet, or even something as small as a drawer. Again, work easiest to hardest. If you're just not sure what to do with something, let it go for now. We'll be getting to your hard choices in the next chapter.

As much as possible, with each new physical space you tackle, create three piles:

1. Things to keep
2. Things to relocate within the home
3. Things to remove

After sorting, return your things-to-keep items to where they belong best. When possible, store these items out of sight, because this will help remove physical distraction. Also, when putting things away, place your most-used items at the front of shelves and relegate your less frequently used things to the back. (That's free organizing advice from me to you.)

Next, deal with your things-to-relocate pile by taking those items to their proper places in your house. For example, if you picked up toys from the hallway, deposit them in the toy box. If you found your teenager's clothes draped over a chair back, they probably belong in the laundry basket. Come to think of it, make her put them there herself.

Finally, sort your "things to remove" pile into four subcategory piles: donate, sell, recycle, and throw away. Then deal with each of these piles in the appropriate way. Don't let them sit any longer than necessary, because if you do, they'll get scattered and turn back into the clutter you're trying to escape.

When tackling any space, it is important to physically touch every item. Almost every professional organizer will give you the same advice because handling an item forces you to make decisions about it. It is too easy to leave items alone if you are only quickly scanning them.

Does the thought of handling every item in your home sound daunting? I hate to say it, but if it does, that's an indication in itself that you own too much. Use that fact as motivation to make quick decisions. If you thought an item was important enough to bring into your home, you can find the strength to decide again if it actually is.

In your process of removing the unneeded excess, you'll want to develop your own working definition of *clutter*. Early in our minimizing journey, my wife and I began to define clutter as (a) too much stuff in too small a space, (b) anything that we no longer used or loved, and (c) anything that led to a feeling of disorganization. Feel free to rip off that definition if you want. But there are other definitions you might find resonate better with your ideals. For example, Joshua Fields Millburn defines clutter as anything that does not "add value" to his life.[1] Marie Kondo describes clutter as those things in her home that do not "spark joy."[2] Peter Walsh goes even further, saying that clutter is anything that "interferes with the life you could be living."[3] And William Morris says it this way: "Have nothing in your house that you do not know to be useful, or believe to be beautiful."[4]

Choose the definition of clutter that works for you, then remove everything that fits the definition.

In some cases, this step will be easy: Your car is littered with things that don't need to be there. A junk drawer is full of unneeded items, such as brittle rubber bands, dead batteries, or keys to locks you no longer own. The top of your dresser has gathered countless odds and ends. Closets are full of clothes you no longer wear. Awards no longer mean anything to you. Decorations are outdated.

In other cases, this step will take more time and intentionality. Think of larger projects, such as the garage, basement, or attic. Functional rooms, including kitchens and offices. Sentimental items accumulated over the years. Items related to your favorite hobbies, arts and crafts, cooking, sports, or music, just to name a few. Other family members' clutter that has begun invading common spaces.

We will cover many of these areas in upcoming chapters. But for now, the most important key in completing this step of removing the excess is to start with the small and easy projects. Begin there. Experience and emphasize small victories.

And now I need to give you a warning.

With all things in life, it is important not to confuse a *desire to* change with *actual* change. *Thinking about* decluttering or *talking about* decluttering won't result in any positive benefits. You can experience these benefits only when you have *actually removed* the excess clutter.

Remind yourself today that talking about change is not the same as implementing change. And take one small step in the right direction because of it.

ELIMINATE REDUNDANCY AND GET RID OF REPETITION

Many people fear that if they remove an item from their home they will regret it in the future. So they keep it "just in case." This is a major cause of clutter, even though we rarely find ourselves needing the thing we have kept "just in case."

If the fear that you will regret removing things is hindering you as you go from room to room to declutter, try this easy method to get around it: get rid of duplicate items. The beauty of eliminating duplicates is that you know there will always be one available "just in case."

To take an example, consider towels. Of course your family needs towels. But you could easily simplify your life by reducing the number of towels you own. For example, maybe you have a family of four, yet you might have a dozen or more towels. In reality, two towels per person—one towel to use, while the other is being washed—is probably sufficient for your needs. You may not be ready yet to live with only two towels per person, but as you think about that stack of towels in your linen closet, don't you think it would be nice to free up some space by removing a few of them?

Do the same throughout your home. You'll probably find duplicates everywhere. The fact is, it is easy to fall into thinking that goes like this: *If owning one of something is nice, owning more will be even better.* So we wind up with multiples. Bowls, bed linens, pens and pencils, spatulas, cooking sheets, cups, clothes hangers, jeans, shoes, coats, coolers, suitcases, shovels, hoses, hammers, computers . . . The litany of the kinds of items that we have too many of is a long one. Sometimes we even own duplicate homes and vehicles!

As you begin removing extras, you will notice something unbelievable. Your home will suddenly be filled with only your favorites of every object. You will also naturally begin to take better care of your belongings, because it will be easier to notice items that need to be repaired or replaced.

Furthermore, almost immediately after eliminating duplicates, you will notice countless other things that can be reduced in your home. Before you know it, you will have made significant progress in your journey toward a simplified life. This is the kind of benefit that will make you want to tell a friend about minimizing—and how it's changing your life for the better.

SHARE YOUR STORY

I remember vividly the days when my two children were born. What parent doesn't? On both birth days, I picked up the telephone and called all of our family members and closest friends to share the announcement with them. The joy in our lives was bubbling over, and I could not wait to include others in the moment. Hearing others get excited made me even more excited.

I learned a valuable life lesson on those occasions: Joy is meant to be shared. It doesn't reach its fullness until we include others in it.

And it's not just the huge moments in life, such as the birth of a child, that we want to share with others. It's the smaller things too. When we find a great restaurant, we recommend it. When we read a fascinating book, we tell a friend. When we discover a shortcut, we suggest others try it.

The practice of sharing good things with others improves their lives by allowing them to discover the same joy we have. It also enhances our lives by confirming our happiness and reinforcing the positives of the course we're on.

So as you begin making changes to simplify your life at home, I encourage you to take the simple step of sharing your story with your friends, family members, coworkers, and neighbors. Look for opportunities, perhaps over coffee, during a meal, or around the water cooler, to talk about your newfound passion for owning less. Try this easy opener: "One thing I've realized recently is that I'm actually happier when I own less. For me, it all started . . ."

You will find that people may be excited to try minimizing for themselves. Even if they aren't, they will cheer you on in your own process of learning to live with less. They will motivate you by holding you accountable and asking how things are going the next time they see you. As an additional benefit, when you share your story, you will be reminded again of the reasons why you decided to declutter in the first place.

START TODAY

These, in review, are the baby steps to owning less:
- Write down your goals.
- Start decluttering with the easy targets in your lived-in areas.
- Then go room by room, tossing out and tidying up.
- Eliminate duplicates as you make your circuit.

- Share your story with others to keep yourself motivated during and beyond the first steps.

I still have much more to say to challenge your assumptions about how much stuff you really need. But for right now, these five steps are all unintimidating, achievable actions that anybody can do. In addition to them, you may think of some other ways to jumpstart your pursuit of a lifestyle that's free from the burden of material excess. Remember, the important thing is that you focus initially on the easy things and not the hard things.

So go ahead. Start your decluttering journey with the easiest step. Before moving on to the next chapter, just pick one drawer or closet—whatever seems achievable—and clean it.

Your first step in the right direction should be an easy one. Take it today.

Troubleshooting

After we've begun decluttering our homes, difficult decisions will inevitably begin to surface. We can't avoid them. As more and more clutter leaves our homes, we eventually stand face to face with those items we have put off until the end. These are the pesky trouble spots in our minimizing process.

In this chapter, I will highlight some of the most common categories of items people have difficulties with as they minimize their homes:

- books
- paper
- technology
- keepsakes
- and two other, less expected topics I'll introduce when the right time comes

I will identify each problem area, make the case for less of each, and provide practical ideas to help you navigate that area. Some sections of this chapter may be more relevant than others to you, but through each of them you'll see a common theme emerge: you're getting back more than you're giving up.

DEATH OF ONE DREAM, BIRTH OF ANOTHER

In a chapter called "The Hardest Thing to Cut" in his book *The 100 Thing Challenge,* Dave Bruno writes about his decision to sell all the woodworking tools from his garage. These were tools that he had accumulated slowly over many years and that he cared about, but they would have to go, given his self-challenge to reduce his possessions to just one hundred things. Throughout the story, Dave makes it clear that he spent as much time daydreaming about his perfect little woodworking shop as he did actually using the tools themselves. He knew they had to go.[1]

Dave located a buyer for the woodworking tools and helped to load them into the man's pickup, then watched the tools leave his life forever. "My woodworking ambitions were put on hold," Dave declared. "In addition to looking at living a year with only one hundred personal possessions, I was no longer pretending to be an artisan on the weekends."[2]

For Dave, the removal of those tools represented the death of a dream. "I'd try to stop daydreaming about being a master woodworker. . . . In real life, I do not fit the profile. . . . It was tough to give up my hope of being someone I am not and not likely to become."[3]

Sometimes, parting with our possessions means giving up an image that we have created in our mind of the person we would like to become. Sometimes, minimizing possessions means a dream must die.

But this is not always a bad thing. It may be difficult in the moment, but it may also be necessary. Sometimes, it takes giving up the person we wanted to be in order to fully appreciate the person we can actually become.

And this is what I want you to remember when you get to the tough spots in reducing your possessions. Often, these tough spots are tough, not just because they're hard to minimize in a practical sense, but also because it seems like we're giving up something important. What we're giving up may not always rise to the level of a dream, but at the very least we're facing the loss of something that seems particularly valuable or important to us.

So the way to get through the tough spots is to remind yourself that what you're heading toward by giving up this hard-to-part-with thing is a greater good. The good that will come from having a life of less will be so much better than hanging on even to those things that seem most dear but aren't really helpful to you.

When you face your own internal resistance about getting rid of something you know that you really ought to let go of, think specifically about how less might be more in that area of your life, and it will usually cut the knot of your indecision.

SHELVED

Less than six weeks after being introduced to minimalism, I received a surprise e-mail at work. It was from our boss. The memo announced a mandatory office clean-out day for the entire staff. A dumpster would be rented. Phones would be turned off. Appointments were to be rescheduled. Lunch would be delivered. And every employee was directed to spend the day cleaning out his or her office and every common area in the building.

Imagine that. Paid to minimize! It was almost too good to be true.

At the time, my office, frankly, was a mess. My desktop, drawers, and shelves all bore an embarrassing amount of clutter. Probably more than any of my coworkers, I needed a day to remove everything that did not really need to be in my office.

On clean-out day, I arrived early and set about removing all the things I did not need in my workspace. At the top of my list: books.

I minimized my book collection from three bookcases to one in the course of that single day, I'm proud to say.

Outdated reference books were the first to go. I reminded myself that I could find most of the information in them faster on the Internet, anyway.

Books that I had never read (and realistically was never going to) were removed next. I felt a sense of relief as they left. No longer would I feel burdened by all the books I "should have read." Instead, I was free to look forward to new reading opportunities.

When thinking of the books I had read, I asked myself whether it was a book I used often or regularly recommended. If the answer was yes, I kept it for future reference. If the answer was no, I removed it from my workspace.

On the same day, I removed framed credentials from my wall, both college degrees and licensing certificates. While I did, it occurred to me that I had hung those items on my walls only for the sake of reputation—a clue to guests that I should be respected.

Then I had another revelation. I had done the same thing with books. A part of my motivation for cramming my shelves with books was to signal to anyone who visited my office that I was well read, intelligent, and worthy of esteem.

Understanding this about myself, I felt embarrassed. And as I removed the two-thirds of my books that I didn't really need, I resolved to no longer seek to impress others by the number of books on my shelves.

How to minimize books is among the top five questions I get asked, and it rarely has to do with work-related books. Instead, the questions come from book lovers. The kind of people who have novels stacked up by their beds, books stuffed in their briefcases for a quick read at lunchtime, and overflowing bookshelves in more than one room of the house.

Whether you have thousands of volumes in your book collection or mere dozens, and whether you bought them for professional reading or for pleasure, you can benefit from trimming the collection. Remember, you've got big plans for your life, and clutter—even intellectual clutter—can get in the way of your accomplishing those plans.

If you recognize books as a problem area for you, here are some helpful thoughts to get you started in thinning out your collection.

- *Realize that books do not define you.* Books add value. They *contribute* to who you are. But they do not *define* who you are, whether in abundance or in lack.
- *Remind yourself that the memory of a book is not the same thing as the book itself.* Sometimes it's the way a book made us feel that keeps us from letting go of it. Often,

taking the time to write down those feelings and those
connections makes it easier to pass along the book to
someone who would love the book as much as we did.

- *Think of forwarding good books as an act of love.* Keeping
a good book on your shelf means you are simultaneously
keeping it from someone else. Share the joy.

- *Set reasonable boundaries for your collection.* Boundaries
help us quickly distinguish the most important from the
somewhat important. They are helpful in countless
pursuits; use them to your advantage. I chose to minimize
my office book collection from three bookcases to one,
but that degree of elimination may be too aggressive for
you at the moment. That's okay. This is not a race.
Choose your own boundaries and give it a try. You can
always adjust later.

- *Give yourself permission to keep your favorites.* Remember, less is different from none. Identify your favorite
books and keep them close. You will find freedom in
knowing that all decisions are coming from you and
nobody is forcing them upon you.

- *Read in pixels rather than print.* With today's e-book
readers, you can store dozens of books on a device far
thinner than a mass-market paperback. If you keep that
many books in your device library, then in a sense you
still have clutter—digital clutter. But it's less distracting,
less burdensome, and easier to access and store than print
books.

GOOD-BYE, MR. PAPER

When I was young, my aunt Sharron gave me a nickname: Mr. Paper. She still jokes about it today, even though the jest has gotten a bit old after thirty-five years. But, at the time, she had a point. I did love paper.

I loved empty notebooks of every kind: blue, yellow, green, one-subject, three-subject, each with a wire binding on the left. I used them to write stories, draw pictures, record statistics, list baseball cards, or do math homework. Most of them I kept in a messy pile on the floor of my bedroom.

As I grew older, I became less infatuated with notebooks. However, I continued to be surrounded by piles of paper. But now they weren't baseball statistics. They were bills to be paid, tax receipts to be filed, coupons to be clipped, work assignments to get to, magazines to be perused, and a never-ending stream of mail to be sorted.

Getting a handle on paper clutter is not easy. And it would be dishonest for me to say I have entirely conquered this tough area. Paper seems to flow into our homes on a daily basis from any number of sources—mail, school, church, and work, to name a few. It is a major cause of clutter in many homes and is a difficult hurdle to cross.

How much paper do you have in your home? Try this experiment: Estimate how many file-cabinet drawers you could fill with the paper in your home. Then do the math. The average file-cabinet drawer will hold 4,500 sheets of paper when full.[4]

A lot, isn't it?

Not that you're likely to have all your paper neatly filed in drawers.

Most of us tend to dither over, stack, and aimlessly move around papers rather than doing something purposeful with them. Even business executives will pick up a piece of paper thirty to forty times before doing something with it.[5]

In addition to the time and physical space it takes to sort, file, and store paper, there is the mental space that paper clutter takes up in our mind. "Clutter is a visual sign of . . . procrastination, and carries with it just as much anxiety," Leo Babauta writes.[6] And never has this statement been more true than when we talk about paper clutter.

Unpaid bills, unread newspapers, unsorted mail, and unfinished work projects clutter our counters and desks and clamor for our attention. Each time we walk past stacks of paper, our minds are distracted from the present motivation in our lives. For this reason, it is important to remove as much clutter as possible from our field of vision and focus on whatever's more important to us.

The opportunity to go paperless—keeping all documents in digital form—is becoming more and more accessible, even for low-tech homes. I would recommend it if your mind works in that way.[7]

But even if you don't decide to go entirely paperless, minimizing paper is still possible. Despite a predisposition against it, I have made great strides implementing some simple processes that are reproducible in any family. The process of removing paper clutter from our homes boils down to answering three questions: *Why? What? How?*

Why?

To get started, ask yourself, *Why do I keep paper?* The answer could be any number of reasons:

- You are a procrastinator, and paper represents decisions you are putting off.
- You are disorganized, and paper clutter is a result of poor filing solutions.
- You are uninformed and keep too many documents because you don't know what you need to keep and what you can throw away.
- You are too busy to handle it or read it, so you store it for later.
- You have a sentimental attachment to paper items such as love notes, children's artwork, and newspaper clippings.

You can't achieve a solution to your paper clutter until you decipher why it collects in your home.

What?

After you discover the *why,* you can more easily answer the question, *What papers do I actually need to keep?*

Before becoming minimalist, I held on to countless financial documents. One look in my filing cabinet would have revealed credit-card statements and utility bills from ten years prior. I kept them because I thought I needed to.

But, in reality, this is not the case. While it is *essential* to review the specific laws in your area, many countries generally require you to keep personal financial records for only three years.[8] And with institutions making more and more financial records accessible online, keeping paper files is becoming less necessary.

When it comes to the nonfinancial or nonlegal paper clutter that seems to collect, adopt a museum mentality for your home. A part of what makes a museum great is the stuff that's *not* on the walls, because that's what makes the featured artwork stand out. So become a curator of items you keep for sentimental or general-reading reasons. Minimize your paper clutter by choosing to keep just your favorites from among your child's artwork, your student's school papers, or the publications you hope to read in the future.

How?

After answering the *why* and *what* questions, you will be better able to establish new habits. Now you need to ask, *How am I going to keep paper clutter under control?*

The two keys are to (1) act quickly and (2) file appropriately.

As paper enters your home, make a decision and act upon it. Throw junk mail away. Clip coupons. Pay bills. Store school records. File financial documents. Each of these acts takes only seconds—minutes at most. Rather than laying papers on a countertop where they can attract more clutter, process them immediately.

Store items you cannot handle immediately in a designated location for further processing (I recommend a simple manila to-do file folder). At a future time, sit down and work through the contents entirely in one sitting, filing or discarding items as necessary.

This simple process of acting quickly and filing at once will work for almost every type of paper clutter in your home. You won't miss the stacks of paper. Instead, you'll love the freedom you feel in being free of paper that distracts you from what you want to be doing.

DEVICE ADVICE

Technology changes fast. And new advancements are announced with great fanfare. The promise of changing how we interact with the world sounds good to us, and so we buy and buy these devices in incredible numbers. Meanwhile, our old devices sit around because we're not sure what to do with them. Is ever-growing device clutter inevitable?

Experts in the tech world make a distinction between *technical obsolescence* and *functional obsolescence*. Technical obsolescence occurs as soon as your device is surpassed in its features by another device of its type. For example, the maker of your smartphone comes out with a newer model six months after you bought yours. Functional obsolescence, on the other hand, occurs only when your device no longer works like it's supposed to. That happens, for instance, when the software it runs ceases to work properly and is no longer supported by the manufacturer.

A lot of us are tempted to buy something new soon after our device reaches the point of technical obsolescence. If we find out that the cool new gadget we bought last month has been replaced on the market by an even cooler one, then we want that new one!

I would argue that we should wait until we get closer to functional obsolescence. So what if we don't have the newest thing? Who's really going to care?

Now, I am not against the development or use of technology. In fact, I'm pleased to say that minimalism is more possible today than ever before because of technology. In my phone, I carry movies, books, music, maps, a calendar, a Starbucks card, and an address book (just to name a few)—all things I don't have to maintain in bulkier formats. Technology is one reason minimalism continues to grow; it has never been easier to own less.

But I fear that these days many people assume new technology automatically makes things better and only adds convenience. This is not true.

In fact, when we don't consume technology in a mindful way, it often adds clutter to our lives. It quickly drains our energy, our time, our space, and our bank accounts. Who among us hasn't wasted an entire afternoon trying to get a computer to accomplish one seemingly simple thing?

When deciding whether to buy new or to hang on to old devices and gadgets—both in the present and the future—the filter we need to employ is the simple question, "What problem does it solve?"

Technology should make our lives easier by solving problems both at home and at work quickly and more efficiently. But if our technology is not solving specific problems for us, it is only adding to them.

Eliminating the clutter caused by holding on to old devices (and their cords and batteries) that we are no longer using is often just a matter of taking the time to dispose of them properly. Most areas have electronics donation and recycling centers.

But what about our future purchases?

Buying a new phone just because the upgrade has become available is foolish if it does not improve your life in a tangible way. The same could be said of cameras, home entertainment equipment, and computers. You don't need a bigger-screen television if you can see fine with the one you currently have. Rarely do people regret waiting as long as possible to upgrade their technology. You don't need to line up to purchase a new product just because the corporation that manufactures it says you need it.

What you need to do instead is count the full opportunity cost of your purchases. What else could you do with the money you won't spend if you pass up a tech purchase? Pay down your debt? Enjoy a weekend vacation? Replace that worn-out mattress you've been using a lot longer than your last phone?

Start asking whether new technology is really improving your life or taking you away from what matters.

Hanging on to technology for a while isn't the end of a dream. It's the beginning of making greater progress toward what you want out of life.

ONLY THE BEST

For my wife and me, decluttering our basement was one of the last steps in our process of minimizing. This was not just because we had so much stored down there (although we certainly did). More importantly, this step was going to be the most emotional one for us. After all, the contents of the boxes we stored in our basement told the stories of our lives. There were high-school yearbooks, college textbooks, and unused wedding gifts. There were shoe boxes filled with photos and souvenirs from trips overseas. There were artifacts preserving count-less memories of childhood. It wouldn't be easy on us to get rid of any of it.

The project would eventually take months and require emotional commitment. But we had trained. After pruning our possessions every-where else in our house, we had solidified our belief that less is better. And so we were mentally prepared to pass our biggest test: deciding which of the sentimental items we had collected over the past twenty years we were going to toss.

We evolved a strategy I call "only the best." It's what I recom-mend to anyone anguished over the prospect of removing some of the objects that have memories attached to them. We didn't get rid of everything, nor did we keep all of it. We kept only the best—meaning the highest quality and most meaningful—items with which to re-member former times and beloved people. Then, instead of keeping those special pieces in boxes, we found places for them in our home where we could see them. This way, our minds were actually drawn back to cherished memories more often.

Let me give an example of what this looked like.

One of the most emotional moments for Kim during our basement-sorting process occurred when we came across the box of mementos Kim had collected from her grandmother Irene's apart-ment after this beloved relative had passed away. In many ways, Irene was a hero to Kim. My wife respected her grandmother's zest for life, her love for family, her passion for prayer, and her commitment to God. So the mementos in this box were dear to Kim. Still, we applied the "only the best" criterion here as elsewhere.

Kim selected three items from the box that, to her, were most representative of her grandmother's life. She selected a candy dish, which now offers a sweet snack to anyone who enters our living room, just as her grandma used it. She chose a butterfly brooch to pin on her jacket, just as Grandma used to wear it when she would visit. And she kept her grandmother's Bible, now residing on our nightstand, just where—you guessed it—her grandmother used to keep it.

In keeping fewer of Grandma Irene's things, we have brought greater value to her memory. More importantly, we have exalted the values that Irene possessed and that we desire to reflect. Because we sorted out the most important from the less important, her legacy lives on even stronger than before.

Are you beginning to see how "only the best" can help you decide what to do with your own archive of stored memories?

If it still seems hard to give some of your keepsakes away, let me give you some tips that may make it easier. Think of these as stops on the way to keeping only the best.

Tip: Try Keeping Half for Now

If paring down the number of your sentimental items is difficult for you, try limiting your sentimental physical items to half their current amount. For example, if you have two boxes of memories from high school, can you cut it down to one?

Getting rid of half is a lot better than getting rid of none. These kinds of self-imposed boundaries often help us quickly realize which items mean the most to us. Eventually we may find it easier to pare down further to only the best items.

Tip: Take Pictures of It Before You Get Rid of It

Are you holding on to some sentimental items because you're afraid you'll miss them? If so, then you may find relief in archiving digital photos of some items before you remove them. Now you've got a record of them, and they are not entirely gone.

Remember, your memories are not stored in the object; the memories are in you. The object only helps you recall them. A photo, therefore, can serve the same purpose as the physical object.

Some people might object to this tip because taking a picture creates something else you're hanging on to—the photo. And true enough, as I said with e-books, digital clutter is still clutter. Yet here again, if organized well, digital clutter is far less intrusive and burdensome than physical clutter. It is easier to move, manage, locate, and access.

So go ahead, take a photograph of the broken-down trunk that your great-grandmother brought over with her on the steamer, the cheap necklace that was the first gift your future husband ever gave you, or your child's first drawing of the human form that actually had a neck. The photograph may turn out to be just as good a memory aid as the item itself.

Tip: Give It Life Again

If you are holding on to sentimental objects that someone else could use, honor your memories by giving those items life again. Donate them in such a way that you can be assured they are creating new memories for others.

The perfect example is baby stuff.

I've noticed that parents have a hard time getting rid of the clothes, toys, and assorted baby gear that their kiddos used. It's understandable. There are precious memories of the irrecoverable baby years associated with those things.

You can keep "only the best" items, such as a baptism gown. But you certainly don't need to keep every rattle, bib, and baby shoe. Your stage in life has changed, and you're making new memories with your kids. In fact, if you keep those things until your kids are teenagers, you're only going to embarrass them with the past.

Besides, there are so many new mothers (single and married) who could be blessed by infant outfits and various kinds of baby paraphernalia. Why do we keep them and selfishly hoard the joy for ourselves? Isn't there even more joy in knowing that those clothes are being worn somewhere else, adorning a precious baby who is being snuggled by her mother right now?

When you give away something meaningful to someone who will appreciate it as much as you did . . .

The recipient will be blessed.

You will be blessed.

And the donated item will be given life again.

We hold on to sentimental possessions because they remind us of what brings joy and meaning into our lives: the people around us, the experiences we share, and the accomplishments of growth and achievement. Unfortunately, too often, the physical possessions we accumulate in our lives keep us from experiencing more of those very things! They burden us with unnecessary stress and care and financial obligation. So don't be afraid to keep only the best of your sentimental objects. You can't reach for new experiences and relationships if you are too busy holding on to yesterday's things.

And now I want to draw your attention to two areas where you might not even have thought about minimizing—but you should. Namely, the vehicle you drive and the home you live in. We're getting to some big-ticket items here. And some high-impact options for giving up a fruitless dream and living a better reality.

PRIDE IN YOUR RIDE

In our society, people (not all, but many) are obsessed with cars. To a point, our interest in cars makes sense. We have built our cities and towns in such a way that living in most communities requires the use of vehicles. But our fascination with vehicles goes well beyond our need for them. They represent far more to us than a means for moving from point A to point B.

Often, car ownership is about status and reputation or size and comfort. We seek to prove our success in society by the cars we drive. I realize there may be other reasons why we buy the cars we do—nostalgia, a love of speed, a fascination with the latest automotive engineering, an attempt to heal some kind of inner wound. But largely we choose our cars for the pride of the ride.

The statistics concerning vehicle use and expense seem to back up the premise that the cars we drive are no longer just about getting from one place to another. According to the American Automobile Association, the average annual cost of owning a vehicle in 2014 was $8,698. For SUV drivers, the cost increases to $10,624.[9] On average, car ownership and operating expenditures make up the second-most significant expense for households (after home ownership), representing 15 percent of annual income. The average auto loan for a new vehicle is over $27,000, and the average used-car loan comes in at almost $18,000.[10] Yet still we really want our nice cars.

Years ago, I spoke at an event in Phoenix on the life-giving pursuit of minimalism. Afterward, a young man approached me and presented his dilemma.

"Joshua, I agree with everything you said. In fact, I live a pretty minimalist life already. But I just have one question. I'd really like to own a nice car. I mean, I *really* want to own a nice car when I can. Is that wrong?"

As he spoke, I was reminded of a quote by syndicated columnist Harvey Mackay that I have repeated on many occasions: "If you can afford a fancy car, you make more of an impact driving an ordinary one."[11]

Here's how I have interpreted Mackay's words: Although you could spend $60,000 on a luxury car to drive around town with style, it's better to spend $30,000 on a more modest, yet still serviceable, car and have $30,000 left to solve a real problem in the world. In the end, buying the $30,000 car actually leads to greater joy and longer-lasting fulfillment.

I invited the young man to consider the fact that he could spend his money and his time on more valuable pursuits than fancy cars. I don't know what decision he eventually made. He was wrestling with the same change of mind-set about car ownership that I would encourage you to make.

We live in the twenty-first century. Unless you live in a location with convenient public transportation, you will likely need to own a vehicle. And I encourage you to get a well-made model from a car-maker with a good reputation. But that doesn't mean you need to own the vehicle that marketing teams are trying to convince you to purchase. You'll be better off owning a vehicle that provides you with the freedom, reliability, and resources to accomplish the greatest amount of good in this world that you possibly can.

When it comes to cars, trading down can actually be trading up if it allows you to pursue things that are more important. In that case, you can have a different kind of pride in your ride.

CASTLE FOR SALE

Just as people in our society tend to buy cars that are much fancier and more expensive than they really need, so they tend to buy houses that are much bigger than they need.

Might you be better off in a smaller home? Let's think this through.

People buy larger homes for a number of reasons: They "outgrow" their smaller one. They start to make more money. A Realtor or lender convinces them that they can afford it. They hope to impress others. Or they think a large home will be their "dream home."

Another reason people keep buying bigger and bigger homes is because no one tells them not to. The mantra of our society again comes calling: *Buy as much and as big as possible, because that is what you are supposed to do when you start making money.*

Nobody gives us permission to pursue smaller rather than larger. And nobody outlines the reasons why we may actually be happier in a smaller house. But the reasons are many.

- *Smaller homes are easier to maintain.* Anyone who has owned a house knows the amount of time, energy, and effort to maintain it. All things being equal, a smaller home requires less from you.

- *Smaller homes are less expensive.* They cost less in both purchase and upkeep (insurance, taxes, heating, cooling, electricity, and so on). This results in more money for other things. And it results in less debt, less risk, less stress, less environmental impact, and less temptation to accumulate more material possessions.

- *Smaller living spaces encourage family bonding.* A smaller home results in more social interaction among the members of the family. And togetherness is good, right?

- *Smaller homes are easier to sell.* This is because they are more affordable for most potential home buyers. And being able to sell quickly when you need to move takes away one of the great stressors associated with owning a home.

When our family moved from Vermont to Arizona, we needed to sell an old home and buy a new one. The housing markets were remarkably different between the two regions, and we could have easily purchased a massive upgrade while still lowering our monthly payments. But we never considered buying a larger home. Instead, we couldn't wait to get into a smaller one.

We still had criteria for our new home. Smaller was not the only goal. Our new house had to function in a way that fit our young family and promoted our values. Our list of nonnegotiables consisted of three bedrooms, a dining room, a family room sufficient for entertaining, pleasant outdoor space, a quality school district in a lovely neighborhood, and high-quality craftsmanship.

We were overjoyed to find a house that fit our desires exactly. We reduced our home size by 30 percent while going from four levels to one level. We reduced our mortgage payments by almost 50 percent; we selected quality over quantity (always a wise decision); we removed the anxiety inherent in burdensome monthly payments; we found a house where every room is in use every day; and we have fallen in love with every square inch of it.

Purchasing a home is a personal decision that requires you to weigh a large number of factors, and I can't address each of them. Only you know all the variables that come into play when making your choice. Yet here's my general advice for you: Choose shelter based on your needs, not what the Realtor says you can afford. Choose an arrangement that will bring freedom, not burdens.

I'm not saying you have to buy a smaller house. I just think you'll be happier if you do. I know we are.

DON'T QUIT

Books, paper, gadgets, keepsakes, cars, and houses are typically some of the toughest areas for people to minimize. In these areas, we think we've got a good reason for holding on to what we've got. *If we give them up,* we wonder, *aren't we giving up something important?*

Actually, we're giving up something important if we *don't* do the hard work of minimizing in these areas. We're giving up the freedom to be able to fully live the life we want. That's the real dream, and it's worth whatever sacrifices we need to make it our reality.

So my final word to you as you turn to face the tough spots for decluttering in your home is this: don't quit.

Years ago, I almost quit writing about minimalism. I had blogged for almost one year and had seen some growth on the site, but nothing too exciting. And so, in February 2009, I simply stopped writing. It was not necessarily a "Nobody reads my blog, I quit!" mentality. Instead, other things started to get in the way. Blogging was pushed to the back of my mind, and I no longer set aside time specifically for it.

My blog—now so much a part of my life—might have faded into digital blackness if it hadn't been for a radio commercial aired on the evening of March 3, 2009.

While driving my car to attend a conference in Massachusetts, I heard on the radio an announcement that a furniture store was collecting old prom dresses to donate to teenagers who wouldn't otherwise be able to afford them. I thought the idea was genius. I still get emotional thinking about teenage girls with no resources being given beautiful dresses for their prom night.

So I returned to my blog with a short post encouraging people to donate old prom dresses. It was my first post in weeks.

Within moments of publishing the post, Christy, a woman I had never met, left a comment: "Come back, Josh." She had been reading my blog from near the beginning, finding inspiration in the ideas, and now she was encouraging me to continue.

Her comment was short. Three words total. But it was encouraging enough for me to carry on with writing and blogging about minimalism. I decided to persevere. I'm so glad I did, because I've found that writing and speaking about the joys of minimalism are part of my purpose and calling.

I know minimalism can be difficult at times. Decluttering a home is both physically exhausting and emotionally draining. A million other things that you could be doing will surface—and you can easily move minimalism to the back burner of life.

But the greatest lessons in life take time and effort. Few people get them right the first time.

In those moments when you want to quit, draw upon the essential life discipline of perseverance. Because you will never reach your fullest potential until you learn to push through the frustration, no matter how difficult your circumstances may be.

Let me offer you a short comment of encouragement: You can do it! I know you can. I've seen people from every walk of life succeed in this journey.

To help you keep going and succeed, in the next chapter I want to share with you a tool for making the hard choices: creating an experiment to gauge whether you can live without something.

Experiments in Living with Less

Have you ever test-driven a car before deciding whether to buy it?

Have you taken home a new household purchase, without being sure you love it, because it came with a money-back guarantee if you weren't fully satisfied?

Has your doctor ever given you a medication for a trial period to see if it helped your symptoms?

I bet you've done all of these things. Most of us have. There are situations where we want to try living with an option before we fully commit to it.

In other words, we experiment with it.

Experimentation is a powerful tool you can use in developing your own expression of minimalism. The idea is simple: if you aren't sure you want to get rid of something, live without it for a while and then decide whether it's necessary to you or superfluous. It's a way of testing your assumptions about how much you need. In my experience, it often proves that we don't need as much as we think.

When people are first pursuing minimizing, I encourage them to try living without things for a set period of time. This helps them make up their minds and push through the difficult phases of minimizing.

But beyond that, minimalism experimentation is a skill that we can use for the rest of our lives. It's like a sensitive gauge that fine-tunes our practice of minimalism.

So what I'm giving you in this chapter is not just a tool that you might want to pick up and use a time or two if it seems valuable. Experimentation is much more important than that. In fact, I would say that the lifelong benefits of minimalism are found here! It's through experimentation that we discover what contentment really looks like and what the other possibilities for our lives really are.

Almost every minimalist I know has put his or her assumptions to the test by experimenting with living with less in various areas. I'll be telling some of their stories later in this chapter. And if you're serious about discovering the more of less for your own life, then let me encourage you to devise your own living-with-less experiments.

The parameters of such an experiment are simple and adaptable.

Experiment: I will live without _____ (possessions) for _____ days (or weeks or months).

At the end of that time I will decide either

    [ ] Yes, I can live without those possessions.

    [ ] No, I still need them.

Based on my decision, I will either get rid of those possessions permanently and not miss them, or I will integrate them back into my life and feel comfortable with that choice.

Nothing else will keep you on your course to minimalism better than experimentation.

How to Know

In my family, we have tried numerous experiments. For example, we canceled our cable-television subscription for a trial period. We turned smartphones into dumb phones by removing apps and notifications. We tried out what it would be like to wear drastically fewer clothes. We didn't eat out for a month. We stopped using our dishwasher. We stored away furniture, cookware, artwork, and children's toys, each time testing out a new limit.

As we conducted experiment after experiment, we began to recognize that our home and family functioned just fine, or even better, without the clutter weighing us down and stealing our time and energy.

But our experiments didn't always yield a yes answer. We didn't always conclude that we should eliminate something permanently.

One such experiment included selling one of our cars to live as a single-vehicle family.

Kim and I had begun to think how much simpler and cheaper it would be to have only one car to maintain, insure, fuel, store, and clean. So, just before leaving Vermont for Arizona, we sold our minivan to a friend, keeping only our Honda Accord as the family vehicle. And then we tried to make the new arrangement work for us. As I recall, we lasted four months. But we knew within the first two weeks that it wasn't really working.

It turns out that with two adults who had their own occupations, and two children who had school and active schedules, all living in a city not known for its public transportation, driving two cars was worth it to us. In this experiment, the burden and complications caused by trying to make do with just one car made living out our purpose more difficult. We bought another car.

But honestly, my experience is that most living-with-less experiments are not like this one. Most of these experiments are successful. In fact, I am confident that if you follow through on this idea of experimentation, you will be surprised and delighted to discover how few possessions you actually need. Additionally, the experiments will be opportunities for you to learn more about yourself, and they will open the door to a style of living that is far less complicated, lighter, and filled with more possibilities than you ever thought you could enjoy.

More than that, you won't have to wonder anymore about whether you should live without something. With almost scientific accuracy, you'll *know* whether you should or not.

And whenever you conduct one of these experiments, you will be discovering what the meaning of enough is to you.

FINDING ENOUGH

More than anyone else, Patrick Rhone has shaped my understanding of the concept of enough.[1] Patrick lives in St. Paul, Minnesota, with his wife and daughter. He is a writer who loves Mac computers, fine pens, art, poetry, and beautifully crafted words. In his book titled *Enough,* he applies the experimental attitude toward finding enough:

> Enough comes from trying things out. It comes from challenging your preconceptions. It comes from having less, trying more, then reducing to find out what is just right. It comes from letting go of your fear of less. It comes from letting go of the false security of more. It also comes from having more, losing it all, and finding out what need really is. Enough is hard work.
>
> To get there, one must let go of what-ifs, conjecture, assumptions, guesses, and half-truths. One must overcome fear, gluttony, self-doubt, and thoughts of grandeur. One must ask hard questions to find harder answers. . . .
>
> But, please keep in mind, even that changes. Just as the wire walker must make slight adjustments to constantly changing conditions, so must you.
>
> The goal, then, is not to find what is, or will be, enough forever. That is impossible. The goal is to discover the tools and strategies you need to find what is enough for you right now and provide the flexibility to adjust as the conditions change.[2]

The concept of enough is a personal discovery that must take into account any number of important factors. But if we never look for it, we will never discover it.

Patrick's image of a tightrope walker sticks in my mind. That's you or me up there on that wire! Most of the time, we lean to the side of having too much. But we don't even know it, because we're so used to leaning that way. Experimenting with living without things enables us to see what it's like to lean toward having too little. I would say that most of us (obviously there are exceptions) have never lived with too little. Only as we do so can we find the right balance in the middle. That place of balance isn't too much and it isn't too little; it's just enough. Experimentation helps us find it.

Take something as simple as shoes. How many pairs of shoes are enough? Most of us don't know. If we're interested in minimalism, we might be tempted to say we only need one pair. But actually, unless you intend to wear your work shoes in the garden or on the basketball court, one pair is probably not enough. You'll need at least two. Maybe three if you want an extra-nice pair of shoes to wear to church on Sunday or to go out somewhere special. Is even three enough, then? Maybe for you it is. Or maybe not.

The point is, most of us have never asked those questions. Instead, we have eight or nine (maybe twenty-eight or twenty-nine) pairs of shoes in our closet and would happily buy another pair that we think we need if we found them on sale.

This is just one small example of why we need to challenge our assumptions about how much we actually need.

I would venture to say that most of us already own more than we need. We passed the point of enough a long time ago. We just didn't realize it. And we never will . . . until we begin to see how little we actually need through experimentation.

One person who was urgently motivated to experiment in finding the meaning of enough for herself was someone I mentioned briefly in an earlier chapter, a friend of mine named Courtney Carver.

PROJECT 333

At the age of thirty-seven, Courtney Carver received the kind of medical diagnosis that all of us dread: she had multiple sclerosis.[3] A million questions began swirling in her mind. And Courtney was not the sort of person to take that challenge lying down. Her new obsession became researching her disease's causes, symptoms, treatments, and success stories.

One thing Courtney quickly learned was that stress could contribute to the progression of her disease and that de-stressing could slow it down.

"When I learned about how stress contributes to not just MS, but many other health issues," Courtney told me, "I knew I had to take action. Stress can come from food, fear, worry, busyness, bad relationships, debt, drama, clutter, and a host of other internal and external factors. I knew these were things I could control."

Courtney quickly realized the most effective way for her to eliminate stress was to simplify her life.

"I thought I deserved nice things because I was working so hard. Shopping, I thought, was my stress reliever. But as I began to look around my house, I started to realize it was just building stress—not just the care and cleaning, but also the debt all my stuff represented.

Once I started getting rid of things, I recognized more and more calm and less and less stress. I wondered what else I might eliminate to find more peace."

Courtney relayed to me a story about the three vases with dried Gerbera daisies—a keepsake from her wedding—she displayed on the bureau in the bedroom she shared with her husband. Courtney remembers looking at the vases one evening and asking herself the question, *Are these vases really benefiting me? It seems all I ever do is dust them.* Without telling her husband, she decided to remove them for sixty days. Toward the end of the experiment, she realized her husband hadn't even noticed they were gone—and neither did she. And so she looked for more places to experiment with less.

In an effort to simplify her morning routine while still maintaining a specific fashion style, Courtney invented a personal experiment called Project 333.[4] For a span of three months, Courtney allowed herself the use of only thirty-three items of clothing—shoes and jewelry included (but underwear, sleepwear, and workout clothing excluded). Indeed, at the end of the three months, Courtney's closet was cleaner, tidier, and filled with only thirty-three items—a number she keeps even today.

Courtney's challenge has since been reported by nearly every major news network and has been accepted by tens of thousands of people, both men and women from all around the world in countless climates. And thanks to Courtney's example, many (including me) are finding freedom from the morning stress of looking into a stuffed closet and finding nothing to wear.

Among other lessons that Courtney's experiments have for us, they remind us that we don't have to give things away immediately. In experimenting, we set things aside temporarily, while we decide what to do with them. Just as Courtney held on to her three vases and her extra clothes until she was sure she didn't need them anymore, so we can put our questionable possessions in storage until we make up our minds about them.

It's not a cop-out. It's a useful strategy. I call it *leveling*.

LEVELING: YOU NEED THIS

One of the first conversations I had about our family's decision to minimize was with Liz, a friend of Kim's and mine. We were in the backyard of a mutual friend enjoying a beautiful New England summer evening when I began to share with Liz about the changes we were going through. I told the story of cleaning my garage and hearing from my neighbor that we didn't need to own all that stuff. Then I happened to mention that we had filled several boxes with our excess things and placed them in the basement until we decided what to do with them.

At this point Liz asked, "Are you minimizing, or are you just leveling? It sounds to me like you're only moving things from one room to another."

That made me stop and think. In a sense she was right: moving excess things into a storage space was hardly the same thing as owning less. It wasn't minimalism, and I had been less vigilant in removing things than I could have been. We don't really gain freedom from possessions until we permanently remove them from our lives.

And yet, looking back, I can see that relocating our stuff to the basement was an important step. It allowed us time and space to make better decisions about the things we would keep and the things we would remove.

Liz had meant her reference to "leveling" as a challenge—a well-intentioned one. But instead of resenting it, I decided to embrace her challenge. Ever since then, I have promoted the advantages of leveling.

Years ago, I was speaking at an event on the life-giving invitation of minimalism and the practical benefits of owning less. After the presentation, a woman in her midtwenties approached me and proceeded to tell me her story.

This young woman had received her college degree and had begun working for a local company in a location-independent role, meaning she could do her work remotely from anywhere in the world. She loved the idea of traveling and of using this season in her life to see the world. But she said, "I have a problem. I have an apartment full of things I am having trouble parting with. I want to travel—I really do. But I am waiting until I can get rid of all my stuff. Can you help me find the motivation to finally minimize all of it?"

As she asked the question, I remembered that warm summer evening and my conversation with Liz. I offered an idea. "If the items are too difficult to part with today," I said, "maybe you could just try leveling for now."

My advice to the young woman was this: "Don't let your possessions stop you from chasing your dreams. Rent the smallest storage unit you need. Put everything inside. Go travel the world. I can almost guarantee, when you return after six months and open up the door to that storage unit, you will not have missed most of it. And finally removing them will be easier than you imagined."

She accepted the challenge. And she now has irreplaceable memories of traveling.

Leveling has become the word I use to describe this intermediate step that many will employ as part of their decluttering journey.

The practicalities of the idea are simple.

If you are not quite ready to part with an object, either for sentimental or functional reasons, place it in a box with similar items. On the outside of the box, write a date and a brief description of the contents. Store the box somewhere out of sight, perhaps in the basement, attic, or back of a closet.

Some months later, when you have forgotten all about it, you will stumble upon the box. When you do, take it out and review the contents. Most likely, you will find it much easier to part with the items within. You will recognize that you don't need the items as much as you originally thought you did.

Additionally, you will find your sentimental attachment to these items has diminished significantly. Objects are not people. Rarely does an object's absence make the heart grow fonder.

Once you've accepted the leveling strategy, apply it where you need to. Another friend of mine, Ryan Nicodemus, shows a radical example of how it can help.[5]

THE PACKING PARTY

Ryan Nicodemus had a fancy title at work, a nice income, a large condo, and a cat. As he put it, "I had everything I ever wanted, everything I was 'supposed' to have. . . . My cat and I were living the American Dream."

Ryan would tell you that, while on the outside things looked good, something was missing. "Even though I earned a lot of money," he said, "I had heaps of debt. . . . Chasing the American Dream cost me a lot more than money: my life was filled with stress and anxiety and discontent. I was miserable. I may have looked successful, but I certainly didn't feel successful. It got to a point where I didn't know what was important anymore."[6]

Unbeknownst to Ryan, his best friend of twenty-five years—Joshua Fields Millburn—had discovered the idea of minimalism while cleaning out the belongings of his recently deceased mother. That life crisis, along with a recent divorce, motivated Joshua to rediscover what mattered most to him. Joshua had spent the last several months not only discarding the possessions of his mother but removing unnecessary possessions from his own life as well.

Over lunch one weekday afternoon, Joshua encouraged Ryan to consider the possibility of owning less. He accompanied the invitation with a simple promise: "Once you get the clutter out of the way, you will find room for what is truly important."

And Ryan decided to do just that.

In one of the most unique ways I've ever heard about . . .

Ryan and Joshua held a "Packing Party."

Over the course of nine hours, Ryan and Joshua packed every-thing in Ryan's three-bedroom condo into boxes. And by "every-thing," I mean *everything*: the kitchen, dining room, living room, family room, all three bedrooms, closets, and overflowing junk draw-ers. They even covered the furniture with sheets.

Ryan's challenge going forward was simple: unpack items only when they were needed.

By the end of two weeks, Ryan was shocked at how much stuff was still packed—not needed or rarely used. This process caused Ryan to reevaluate his priorities and life in significant ways.

Several weeks into his experiment, he summed up his findings like this: "Have you ever stopped to think about where your beliefs come from? The house we all believe we need to have, the 2.5 children we believe we need to create, the two cars we believe are necessary to live the American Dream. I'm not sure where all of mine came from, but I am beginning to rethink them. I am finding out that my condo, the stuff in it, and the boxes I have packed up are not as important as I once believed they were. I packed a lot of things that I truly believed I needed to keep. I believed it deep down. And yet here are the major-ity of the boxes. Just sitting here. Unpacked. Unused."[7]

You don't need to go to the extent with leveling that Ryan did. You don't need to pack up everything. But don't hesitate to box up and set aside anything you think you might be able to live without. That's the intermediate zone in your experimental approach to getting rid of what you don't need and improving your life.

FREEDOM IS TWENTY-NINE DAYS AWAY

As we've seen, there are lots of ways to go about creating a living-with-less experiment. Let me give you a suggestion you can use with any of them: include the number twenty-nine.

When Kim and I were carrying out experiments to find out what we could live without, we often gave these experiments a term of twenty-nine days. Why was that? Well, twenty-nine days just somehow seemed a manageable amount of time. It wasn't quite a month, in the sense that an item on sale for $9.99 seems more affordable than the same item priced at $10.00. Yet twenty-nine days was a substantial amount of time, sufficient in most cases for us to make up our minds on whether we wanted to keep something or not.

Our friend Liz was right—we didn't want to leave things boxed up in our basement forever. Better to haul them away to a charity receiving dock sooner rather than later if we weren't going to use them ourselves. We needed a termination date. Twenty-nine days just had a nice sound to it for us.

Is the number twenty-nine magical? Of course not. And yet . . . if it enables you to define your own experiments, make them manageable, and actually get them done, then yes, it *is* magical!

If you can live happily without it for twenty-nine days, very likely you can live happily without it forever.

So . . .

whatever type of possession you want to try living without . . .

whatever number of items, or percentage of items, you want to try either removing or restricting yourself to . . .

however long you want your experiment to last . . .

. . . establish those parameters specifically, mark the end date on your calendar, and get started.

If you are wondering about practical suggestions, I've got some for you.

Clothes

Most of us have closets full of clothes we no longer wear or even like. They are just taking up space. So consider your closet a prime place to start getting serious about living with less. Could you function just fine wearing only 50 percent of your clothes, or even 25 percent? I bet you could. And I bet you'll find getting ready to be much easier when you love everything hanging in your closet.

Courtney Carver wore only thirty-three articles of clothing for three months. You could try her approach.

Or even simpler, use the "magic-twenty-nine" rule:

Experiment: I will remove twenty-nine items of clothing from my closet and will dress without them for twenty-nine days.

Decorations

If you're like most people, many of the decorations in your home hold no personal value for you. They just happened to match your color scheme or were on sale when you walked into a store. Unfortunately, they are distracting you and your guests from the decorations in your home that do highlight your values or that have a personal story attached to them.

Take a moment to walk through your home with a discerning eye. Remove the decorations that clutter rather than enrich your living experience. You will enjoy having a home that shares your family story in a less-cluttered, more-focused way.

Experiment: I will remove twenty-nine decorating items (or an estimated 29 percent of decorating items) for twenty-nine days.

Toys

Whenever I hear parents complain that their young kids have too many toys, I want to respond by asking, "How do you suppose that happened? Your child isn't driving himself to the store to buy them. If there are too many toys in your house, you are the one to blame." But I'm usually too nervous to say it out loud, so I just think it.

Still, I believe there is great benefit to owning fewer toys. Children will express more creativity, develop longer attention spans, and gain deeper respect for the toys they do own.

Although you may want to consult your children before you relocate their unused toys, there's a good chance that after only a few weeks they will forget the old, unused toys. *You'll* think of them, however, every time you realize that you no longer need to pick them up!

Experiment: I will remove an estimated 29 percent of my children's toys, and for twenty-nine days I will keep track of which of the removed toys (if any) the kids ask for.

Kitchen Utensils

We never seem to have enough storage space in our kitchens. Yet most of our grandmothers cooked more often, more elaborately, and better than many of us today—in smaller, less equipped kitchens.

The truth is that, when it comes to cooking, simple is almost always better. We need far fewer cooking utensils than we currently own. Try removing twenty-nine things from your kitchen, then store them in a plastic bin for the next twenty-nine days. And see if you enjoy cooking more in your new, clutter-free kitchen environment.

> **Experiment:** I will store twenty-nine kitchen utensils and cook without them for twenty-nine days.

Furniture

It may require some heavy lifting, but if you're up for the challenge, removing excess furniture from your rooms will immediately open up significant space and airflow in your home. The rarely used pieces of furniture in your home are taking up more room than you realize.

Sure, this experiment requires you to have a place to store your furniture during the trial period, but it is a way to eliminate some of the largest clutter from your home and make a noticeable difference right away.

> **Experiment:** I will remove at least one piece of furniture from each of the major rooms of my home and put them in storage for the next twenty-nine days.

Instead of spending your next twenty-nine days wondering how you can acquire more possessions, maybe you could improve your life by spending that time determining how much you can live without.

THE ROYAL EXPERIMENTER

According to the Bible, King Solomon of Israel amassed a fortune dwarfing that of any other ruler of his time. Through tribute money from dependent kingdoms, Solomon collected 666 talents (about twenty-five tons) of gold each year. If gold is $1,000 per ounce, that's $800 million every year! And that didn't include his income from taxation and commerce.[8]

He made tons of money (literally), and he spent it too.

In a way, King Solomon did the opposite of the kind of experimentation we've been talking about in this chapter. Instead of seeing how he felt about living with less, he tried to find out what it was like living with more. He said to himself, "Come now, I will test you with pleasure to find out what is good."[9]

Here's how he later summarized his "maximalist experiment":

I undertook great projects: I built houses for myself and planted vineyards. I made gardens and parks and planted all kinds of fruit trees in them. I made reservoirs to water groves of flourishing trees. I bought male and female slaves and had other slaves who were born in my house. I also owned more herds and flocks than anyone in Jerusalem before me. I

amassed silver and gold for myself, and the treasure of kings
and provinces. I acquired male and female singers, and a
harem as well—the delights of a man's heart. I became greater
by far than anyone in Jerusalem before me.[10]

He took this experiment to the limit, saying, "I denied myself
nothing my eyes desired." [11]

And what were the results of his experiment? At the end of his
life, Solomon wrote these words in his journal. You can almost hear
the disillusionment in his voice:

When I surveyed all that my hands had done
> and what I had toiled to achieve,
everything was meaningless, a chasing after the wind.[12]

Futility. That's what Solomon found.

What's interesting to me is that Solomon's is the kind of experimentation that most people today are trying to do (albeit on a much
smaller scale). They too are spending as much money on themselves
as they can. And like Israel's richest king, they are headed toward a
sense of disillusionment and futility.

Let's take heed, why don't we? Let us go the other way and experiment in living with less. As we find out how much we really need to
live and then stick there, I believe we'll make room in our lives for all
the satisfaction and fulfillment that wealthy Solomon was hoping for
but failed to find.

A Tool That Never Wears Out

I am often asked, "How do I tell the difference between a need and a want?"

My answer is always the same: "You'll know if you try doing without something for a while."

Now *you* know how to create experiments that will tell you what to remove from your home and what to hang on to. If you have a family, and if your family dynamics allow it, include your family members in these experiments. If it's just you carrying out the experiments, that can work too.

The important thing is to do it. Don't overthink it. Don't delay it. Don't worry about it. Go ahead with it.

It's just an experiment, after all.

If it doesn't work, quit and try another experiment.

Living-with-less experiments will be most useful to you early on, when you're trying to reset your material lifestyle at a lower, more sustainable level. But even after you've been enjoying a simpler way of life for years, you might want to occasionally carry out an experiment to adjust your approach or help you adapt to new conditions of life. For example, once my wife and I are empty nesters, I bet we'll finally be able to get by with just one vehicle. At the very least, you can bet we'll test it out for twenty-nine days!

Challenge yourself to identify the unneeded things in your home. You'll feel free and light when you discover how few things you really need to live a happy and fulfilled life.

Maintenance Program

If you've been following my advice as you've been reading, you started your minimizing by doing the easy stuff—getting rid of the items in your home that you obviously didn't need. Then you moved on to tackle the harder areas of your home, moving methodically room by room. Along the way, you picked up the skill of experimenting by living without something to determine whether you really need it or not.

Eventually you're going to get to a point where you have your possessions reduced to the number that's right for you, a minimum that allows you to maximize the important values in your life.

That's fantastic.

But how are you going to make it stick? How are you going to keep the clutter from coming back?

I have an answer: start at once to form habits that will help you hold on to your gains.

In any area of life where people are trying to change bad habits, it's wise advice to not just quit doing something harmful but to put a different and better behavior in its place. To take a small example, people who are trying to stop smoking often take up gum chewing. If they didn't pick up this replacement behavior, they might find themselves right back where they started in their nicotine addiction.

Nature abhors a vacuum. Something always rushes in to fill it. Human nature, it seems, is the same.

If you don't want to find yourself filling up the empty spaces in your home that you have just decluttered, then establish practices that will not just get you where you want to be with minimalism but will keep you there too. Like dieters who have reached their goal weight, establish a maintenance program to keep your lifestyle minimal.

I want to suggest five habits that anyone can adopt to consolidate the advantages of minimalism. I'm going to teach you . . .

- daily and weekly routines that can keep your home looking fresh;
- a surefire way to break the hold that stores have on you;
- the single most helpful change you can make in your leisure time;
- what to do about the danger zones of Christmas, birthdays, and other gift-giving occasions; and
- how to turn around and look from a different perspective at what you already own.

I'll start with ten of the easiest and most helpful practices you can incorporate into your schedule to make your home a haven of peace and order every day. These are ones my family practices regularly. I can assure you they work.

CLUTTER BUSTERS

Some people who are feeling overwhelmed about the clutter in their homes think the solution is relying on containers and other organizing tools. While I dismissed that misconception back in chapter 2, a similar misconception is that tidying up will take care of the problem. Clean up the mess and put stuff back where it started, and they've taken care of the situation, they think.

The truth is, tidying up isn't nearly enough to get our households in a state where they no longer burden us. For that, we have to minimize—actually reduce the amount of stuff in our houses. We have to de-own.

Nevertheless, once you've got your house minimized the way you want it, tidying up can keep it there.

The trick is to incorporate tidying practices into your normal routines so that the clutter never has a chance to return. You'll find that tidying up is not hard or burdensome. After all, if you've minimized, there's not nearly as much to put away. Every item has a purpose and every item has a home.

1. *Make your bed each morning.* Mess attracts mess. One of the easiest places to see this is the bedroom. Your bed is the centerpiece of the room, and if it is left unmade, clutter begins to accumulate around it. The first, best step when cleaning a bedroom, then, is to make the bed. And the first, best step for everyday clutter-free living is to make the bed first thing in the morning.

2. *Wash dishes right away.* Hand washing some dishes takes less time than putting them in the dishwasher. This applies to cups, breakfast bowls, dinner plates, and silverware. If you hand-wash right after eating, it will

take hardly any time at all. If, however, hand washing is
not an option, be sure to put used dishes in the dishwasher right away. Nobody likes walking into a kitchen
with dishes piled up in the sink or on the counter, and it's
even less fun eating in there.

3. *Fill your recycling containers and garbage containers.* Use
every trash pick-up day as an excuse to fill your recycling
receptacle and garbage can. Grab a box of junk from the
attic, broken toys from the playroom, spoiled food from
the pantry, outdated paperwork from the office—
whatever has built up. Then put it where the trash person
will pick it up. You'll quickly get the hang of this. You
may even begin to look forward to trash day. (Okay,
maybe I shouldn't go that far.)

4. *Always leave room in your coat closet.* There's a good
reason why coats, boots, and outerwear end up scattered
throughout your home. It's because your coat closet is so
full that it's a hassle to put things away and retrieve them
quickly. So leave room on the coat-closet floor, on the
hangers, and on the shelves for members of your family
to quickly put away or retrieve items.

5. *Keep flat surfaces clear.* Kitchen counters, bathroom
counters, bedroom dressers, tabletops, desktops—these are
areas that just naturally collect clutter. Put small kitchen
appliances away. Scoop up coins. File receipts. Stick
toiletries in a medicine cabinet. Keep an eye on your flat
surfaces and dive in as needed to keep them clean.

6. *Complete one- to two-minute jobs immediately.* Clutter is often a result of procrastination—decisions put off or small jobs left unfinished. Counteract this procrastination in your home with a simple rule: if a job can be completed in less than two minutes, do it now. Take the garbage out, scrub the pot, return the remote control, or place your dirty clothes in the hamper. Every time you see a task all the way through to completion, you've forestalled the development of clutter.

7. *When you finish a magazine or newspaper, process it immediately.* Good recipe in there? Put it in your recipe box and recycle the rest. An article that your husband will enjoy? Clip it and recycle. Coupon too good to pass up? Cut it out and recycle. Stacks of magazines and newspapers serve little purpose but to clutter a room.

8. *Place junk mail immediately into a recycling bin.* Take note of the natural flow of mail in your home. Placing a recycling container near your mail drop-off zone can catch most of that junk mail so it won't even reach your counter. And as an added bonus, you'll begin to look through less of it and therefore be less enticed by the advertisements to buy what you don't need.

9. *Take care of clothes immediately.* When it came to clothes, I used to be a throw-them-on-the-floor guy. Now I handle each item right when I take it off. Dirty clothes down the laundry chute. Clean clothes back to the hanger or drawer. That's it.

10. *Nightly, return items where they belong.* Tell your kids to put their toys away at the end of every day. You need to do the same with the items you're responsible for. Just make a sweep of the house, grab whatever misplaced items you see, and stash them in their places. Do this every night without fail, and it will allow you to begin each morning in a house that's fresh, clean, and clutter-free.

Next, to prevent having more to tidy up than necessary, erect a barricade on the shortest route between you and overconsumption: the road to your favorite store.

GIVE YOUR WALLET A REST

Sarah Peck was struggling to stay afloat financially. She had a graduate degree in architecture from an Ivy League school, but living in San Francisco with an entry-level job and high rent, Sarah had few dollars left over at the end of the month.

Furthermore, she was dismayed by how much money she and her friends were spending to keep up their image in a clothes-conscious society.

"When I thought about it," Sarah said to me, "I realized that $400 outfits like those shown on the covers of magazines can add up to a lot of money. If one were to wear a new outfit every day for a month, that's $12,000 just on clothes. You might think I'm joking, but I know people who have $20,000 to $30,000 in credit card debt from clothes shopping alone. The image pressures on females can be intense."

So, over the course of the year, Sarah thinned out her closet and pared down to a few favorite items. She made more than twenty trips to charity with bags of clothes and gently worn shoes she no longer needed.[1]

But that wasn't all. She also decided to stop buying new clothes for an entire year. This wasn't an experiment like the ones we looked at in the last chapter. Sarah was already convinced that she could live without new clothes for a year. Instead, this was her way of trying to make a complete break with her old clothes-buying habits and establish healthier, more responsible buying habits.

Sure enough, the no-clothes-buying period shifted her outlook on life. It helped to cement her commitment to minimalism.

"By simply refusing to buy new clothing," she recalled, "I began to feel empowered. This is my life and I can live it how I desire. I began seeing some extra money available at the end of the month. I found new freedom to spend it (and my time) on the things I truly wanted in my life. I had resources available to spend time with friends and be involved in athletic endeavors—both things I desperately love."

Sarah Peck's twelve-month shopping moratorium on clothing changed her entire view of what's most important in life. Others I know have instituted other kinds of shopping bans for themselves. For example, Katy Wolk-Stanley determined to not buy anything new (other than underwear and perishables) and to date has lived this way for more than eight years.[2] Assya Barrette spent two hundred days not buying anything new.[3] Cait Flanders spent an entire year buying nothing except groceries and consumables; she even refused to buy takeout coffee during her experiment.[4] Speaking of food, Jeff Shinabarger and his wife once went seven weeks without buying any food (except milk), choosing instead to see how long they could last eating just the food already in their home. It's forever changed how they buy groceries.[5]

As I speak to people from around the country, I'm realizing that self-imposed shopping bans have become so common that they have almost reached the level of a trend. All kinds of people are deciding not to buy for a while so that they can reset their shopping patterns.

I encourage you to do the same. Find freedom through a shopping ban. It will break the cycle of unnecessary shopping in the short term and lay the groundwork for greater victory in the long term.

And then, in our desire to avoid backsliding into excess and clutter, there is another life change available to us that is easy to implement and quickly yields major benefits. In fact, almost everyone I have ever met who made the change recommends it.

Watch less television.

BREAKING THE HYPNOTIC SPELL

Television is like a one-eyed Svengali hypnotizing its viewers into doing what it wants. Through its frequent commercials, it relentlessly tries to persuade us to buy things we don't need. Through many of its programs, it glamorizes wealth and lavish lifestyles. Other forms of media, such as online ads, entice us to overspend as well. But there's still nothing to equal television for promoting the kind of consumerism that we saw in chapter 4 to be so toxic. We have to turn our gaze away from this unblinking eye we've invited into our homes.

Now, again, less is not the same as none. So put down your defenses. I'm advocating watching less television—not doing without it completely. I realize that some TV can be educational and that entertainment is not necessarily an exercise in futility. We still have one television set in our house that we watch occasionally as a family. But I do watch far less—and I think you should too. There are practical ways to go about this.

It may seem easier to make sweeping generalities such as "I'll stop watching TV forever starting today." But for me, at first, it was easier to just pick some specific shows I could easily live without. When we started to experience the benefits of living life rather than watching it, it became easier to cut out even more.

Starting today, make a list of shows you could easily live without. Or even better, think of the one or two shows you really *do* want to watch, and limit yourself to them for the next twenty-nine days.

Another step is to limit the number of televisions in your house. Before we discovered minimalism, we had four TVs in our home. But now I'll never go back to more than one. When we took the TV out of our kitchen, I began to discover how much I enjoyed cooking. And removing the TV from our bedroom reminded me how much I enjoyed . . . (the rest of this sentence has been deleted at the insistence of my wife).

If necessary, go it alone in reducing your TV-programming consumption. Your family members may not be ready to reduce their television viewing. Or they may not be feeling as challenged in this area as you are. That's okay. Make the change in your own life first. To paraphrase Gandhi, become the change you wish to see in your family.

Trust me, it will get easier over time. Television is a self-propagating habit. It promotes its own interests by boldly declaring the Best New Show, the Most Watched Network, the Can't Miss Episode, or the Game of the Year. TV's advertisers routinely play on our fear of missing out by telling us, "Everyone is watching!" But as you commit to watching less, you will be less persuaded by these claims because you will see them less often. Quickly you will realize that you aren't really missing much.

Watching less television just may be your quickest shortcut to better living right away.

RESTORING SANITY TO GIFT-GIVING OCCASIONS

Gift giving is a lovely tradition, spreading joy and creating memories. It brings people together. I respect gift giving as a love language and do not want to rob others of it. And I like getting gifts as much as the next person. But, oh boy, have we gone overboard with it as our society has become more affluent.

Think about all the gifts that are given and received in the course of a year. The average holiday shopper in America spends about $800 on gifts during the Hanukkah/Christmas season.[6] In addition, most of us receive several presents for our birthdays. And then there are all the other gift-giving occasions throughout the year, such as

Valentine's Day, Easter, Mother's Day, Father's Day, Grandparent's Day, and even Boss's Day. And don't forget special occasions including wedding anniversaries, baby showers, housewarmings, graduations, recoveries from sickness or surgery, thank-yous, baptisms or confirmations, and bar and bat mitzvahs.

If there's the slightest chance of justifying a gift purchase, you can be sure there's a retailer somewhere who's promoting it.

It's enough to make us minimalists throw up our hands and cry, "Stop the madness!"

What are we going to do to avoid getting gifts we don't want from cluttering up our now-minimized homes? It's tricky, because there's the gift giver's feelings to consider. But I believe it's still possible to establish ground rules for the number and kind of gifts we prefer to receive.

- *Make your gift requests known early.* Though it does not always work out this way, gift givers should desire to match their gifts with the recipient's wishes and lifestyle. Creating gift lists and providing them to family members well in advance of holidays, birthdays, and celebrations can be a helpful tool in limiting the clutter collection. Try to provide a wide range of gift ideas varying in price. Follow this formula: request quality over quantity, needs over wants, and experiences over products.

- *Request donations to charities.* Of course people want to give gifts and show their love in a practical way. But this does not necessarily mean they need to purchase something for you to take home. One trend is to request donations to a charitable organization in lieu of physical gifts. You might like to try this, if you haven't already. It feels great to know that the money that could have gone toward a new sweater you don't need instead went to a school scholarship that changed the life of a child in another country.

- *Be patient with your family.* If living with less is a new pursuit for you, do not expect everyone else in your family to understand it the first time around, especially if you have been known for going through various phases in the past. Eventually, they will begin to understand that this is a lifestyle you are seeking to embrace for the long term, and their gift-giving habits will likely evolve.

- *Purge guilt-free.* It may take some time for you and your family to sort out which gifts add value to your home and which only add clutter. With kids, it can often take months to determine which toys are a passing fad and which will become truly beloved. Give it some time. But as the value of the gifts begin to reveal themselves, eliminate the unwanted ones without feeling guilty about it. Especially if they will find more use given to someone else, don't hesitate to give them away. If the giver finds out about it, he or she should realize that regifting is within your rights, since the gift was given without strings attached.

- *Reciprocate your request.* You hope, desire, and expect other people to give gifts that align with your desires.

Return the sentiment when you give gifts to others. Just because you make a desperate plea for experiences over products, for example, does not mean that your brother, sister, father, or mother is requesting the same. If they would like new shoes, consider buying them new shoes. If they make it clear that they desire a department-store gift card for their birthday, consider giving it. Giving gifts is an opportunity to show your love and appreciation. You can make your case for anticonsumerism at a different time.

A DISCIPLINE THAT'S A JOY

If we want to recalibrate to a lower level of accumulation and stay there, we need to replace our culturally inspired greed with self-cultivated gratitude about what we have.

You don't have to have a lot to be grateful. I've been to developing countries all over the world and have seen how poor people live. Many of them are almost unimaginably poor by American standards. Yet I have met grateful, contented people in some of the poorest neighborhoods I have encountered.

On one occasion in the city of San Salvador, I sat in the one-room home of Lucilla and her two daughters, ages fifteen and three. The family lived with almost nothing, surviving on only the money generated from the sale of eggs laid by the six chickens living in their backyard. And yet the hospitality and generosity I encountered in their home was among the most gracious I have ever felt.

Gratitude is a possibility for all of us. It is a choice we can make every day regardless of our circumstances.

Realistically, however, I know there are some seasons when gratitude can be easier. When your home is warm, when you are eating a delicious meal, when your child's report card is impressive, when everything is lining up as you envisioned, it is easy to be thankful. But at other times gratitude appears elusive. When the storms of life hit, thankfulness doesn't come quite so quickly. And yet those are the days when we need it most, because that's when its strength, optimism, and perspective carry us through.

Consequently, gratitude is more valuable to us as an intentional habit than as a spontaneous response. And so it's a good thing that gratitude is an attitude we can cultivate through attention and discipline. It requires practice when it's easy and even more practice when it's difficult. The more we train ourselves to that end, the more we are able to access it when we need it.

Did you know that gratitude improves our overall well-being? Scientific studies over and over again confirm what we already expect to be true: grateful people are happier people. "Gratitude helps people feel more positive emotions, relish good experiences, improve their health, deal with adversity, and build strong relationships."[7] Additionally, those who display a high level of gratitude are much more likely to have below-average levels of materialism.[8]

Gratitude is a discipline, not an emotion. Work hard to develop this habit in your life. Consider these helpful thoughts to spur yourself on in this new discipline of the heart:

- Look for simple joys and be thankful for them.

- Reflect on the good things in your past (particularly if
  your current season of life is a stormy one).
- Find a few minutes in your day to record your gratitude in
  a journal.
- Express thankfulness during life's little inconveniences
  (sitting at red lights, waiting in line, and so on).
- If you pray, begin each prayer with specific words of
  thankfulness to God.

Gratitude helps us better understand our place in the world. It
pushes our praise to those who deserve it. It causes us to focus on the
good things we have, regardless of our present circumstances. It improves our well-being in almost every regard. As a result, it is a sure
pathway to contentment.

WANTING LESS

Owning less is great. But I've discovered that there's something even
better: wanting less. Maybe you've discovered the same thing.

What a great feeling it is when we realize that the desire for more
stuff really has lost its hold over us! Like the Wizard of Oz, consumerism has told us, "Pay no attention to that man behind the curtain!"
But we've peeked behind the curtain, and we've seen that material
accumulation is not nearly what it's been touted to be. We can do better without it. No one can talk us into going back to the old ways.
We'll settle for nothing less than less.

We've got new values and new habits to go along with them:

- Refresh your home by tidying it up every day.

- Impose your own experimental shopping ban.
- Watch less television.
- Bring greater intentionality to your gift-giving rituals.
- Practice gratitude as a discipline.

These are five easy ways to establish helpful new habits that will crowd out the bad old habits that left you burdened. I advise you to try all five of them—and any other habits you can think of that will make minimalism not just an experiment but a lifestyle for you.

If you live with family members, then there's one other necessity to rooting minimalism permanently in your life: you've got to figure out how to bring them along on your journey to having less and loving it. I'm about to show you how.

10

The Minimalist Family

When I speak about minimalism to groups, I love taking questions from people who are just beginning to absorb the topic or are new converts to this way of life. I've gotten so that I know what kinds of questions to expect. Some of the most heartfelt questions I receive are about families. They usually sound something like this:

- "Joshua, you've got me sold on minimalism, but my wife [or husband] is never going to go along with getting rid of a bunch of our stuff. It's almost pointless to try to be minimalist on my own. How am I going to convince my spouse?"

- "We've got little kids at our house. They aren't even going to understand what the word *minimalism* means. They just know they like having a ton of new toys all the time. I can hear the screams now if I try to take their stuff away from them. Can you help?"

- "My daughter's turning seventeen. She's totally into clothes and having the same stuff all the other teenagers have. Wouldn't it be cruel to try to make her different from the rest of the high schoolers? Besides, isn't it too late to start minimizing with her, since she's going to be leaving home before long anyway?"

Any of those concerns sound familiar to you?

If you've got a family, I know how urgently you want to get your family in agreement about minimalism so that you can work toward a simpler lifestyle together. Even if you only *hope* to have a family at some point, this chapter should be helpful to you.

My encouragement to you is rooted in years of working with families much like yours, and it is this: you *can* enlist your family in living a minimalist lifestyle together. Not only can your whole family agree on a goal of living with less, but they can actually be excited about the changes that lie ahead. It might take some time, but getting there is a process of educating the rest of your family, talking things out, and taking practical steps as you advance along the minimalist way together. In this chapter I'll show you how, whether your biggest concerns about family minimalism have to do with your spouse, your young child, or your older child.

And throughout it all, my perspective will be one that you may not have thought about before: *sharing minimalism with your family is an act of love!*

Just as you find minimalism freeing and life giving, so will your spouse and kids. They too can become less stressed, more content, and better positioned to pursue their dreams. Isn't that what you want for them? Sharing minimalism is one of the greatest things you can ever do for them.

Don't let yourself be daunted by the challenges. Let your love for your family motivate you. Start now to help your family receive the gift of a simpler, more fulfilling way of life.

PARTNERS IN LESS

People who choose minimalism as a lifestyle may face any number of doubters. These could be friends, colleagues, or parents. But what do you do when the biggest doubter of all is usually your biggest supporter? What happens next when your partner doesn't support the new you? The fact that you live together only complicates the issue. After all, you share living space—and so does your stuff.

First, talk. Explain what minimalism is and why it attracts you. Share this book with your partner. Describe your vision for how minimalism can be good for the two of you. Make it clear that you are encouraging minimalism, not as an attack on or criticism of the other, but because you love your partner and think minimalism will be good for him or her too. Then listen to what your partner has to say in return.

Be careful about when and how you initiate this conversation. Too often, our conversations about clutter arise from frustration, so they manifest themselves as attacks on the other person. The moment when you are upset that a closet is too full or a drawer won't shut is not the right time. Instead, find a quiet moment when you are drinking coffee or out eating dinner to share what you have been learning and how you think it would benefit your home. Always focus on the benefits and the positive changes that could come from it.

And remember, the minimalism conversation is really not one conversation at all. It's almost always many conversations. So even if your partner seems resistant, keep talking about it in a calm, reasoned manner. After you clear up some misunderstandings and work out some differences, you may find that your partner begins to catch the vision.

In the meantime, resist the temptation to remove your partner's belongings without permission. Start with your own stuff, and minimize as much as you can without treading on shared territory. You may be surprised how much clutter you can remove from your home just by getting rid of your own things.

Your actions to simplify your possessions are not a workaround to try to initiate minimalism in defiance of your partner. Rather, they are another way of presenting the benefits of minimalism. Actions speak louder than words, so allow the benefits of your clutter-free life to do their own convincing. A clean, clutter-free side of your shared closet will be more convincing than an explanation of the 80/20 principle. A refreshingly stress-free desktop or nightstand will begin to look attractive to your partner the first time he or she misplaces something important.

Modeling is an important tool. Don't overlook it. Often we fall into thinking that it is having no positive effect and we'd be better off just imposing our will. But be patient and keep doing what you can on your own to live with less. It may pay off. A woman once shared with me that it took *five years* of modeling minimalism before her husband started to catch on to the benefits. You can't rush modeling; you can only provide it consistently day after day.

As time goes on, you will find common ground for taking steps toward minimalism. Likely, there are some commonly used areas in your home that you can both agree need decluttering. Whether you're targeting a junk drawer, a linen closet, the kitchen counters, or the garage, even the worst of hoarders can typically come to the conclusion that something can be cleaned out (no matter how small the area). Ask your partner about specific areas in your home that you would like to declutter. For example, ask, "Can we both agree there is too much stuff in this bathroom drawer?" Start there, and you may be surprised how supportive he or she can be when you get specific about what you would like to accomplish.

If you find that your partner is slow to make progress toward minimalism, and meanwhile you are pining for the space and freedom that owning less can afford, then try to find one room (or even one corner of a room) to adopt as your minimalist sanctuary. This can be an area entirely free from clutter, noise, and distraction. Spending time in this space will calm you and recharge you to be the best partner and parent you can be. Protect this space. And make the most of it while you wait for your partner to join you on the journey.

THE BATTLE OF THE JELL-O MOLDS

When my wife and I decided to become minimalist, we agreed to pursue this new lifestyle together. But that doesn't mean it has all been smooth sailing since then. We've had plenty of disagreements along the way about how much stuff to unload, how much stuff to keep, and how our purchasing habits should change.

From the very beginning, if I wanted to get rid of 80 percent of our stuff, my wife wanted to get rid of 60 percent. This meant that the first several waves of minimizing went well, but eventually, as I wanted to keep downsizing, my wife began to push back.

I learned a memorable lesson about our differences on August 22, just four months into our journey. I remember the exact date because it was our son's birthday and we had planned a sports-themed party for him. The week before, unbeknownst to my wife, I had taken the liberty to clean out a kitchen drawer. In doing so, I had thrown out the sports-themed Jell-O molds that she was planning to use for the party. The tone of her yell from the kitchen signaled her disappointment unmistakably.

The insight I learned that morning about minimizing with a family is one I have held close to my heart ever since: It is easier to see everyone else's clutter than it is to see our own. Forcing minimalism upon them by removing something without permission is never a good idea. Instead, it is wiser to focus on minimizing our own things before venturing into other people's stuff or even shared family possessions. (I also learned that five-year-olds are just as content with football-field-shaped Jell-O as they are with other sports-themed shapes, though my wife might dispute that.)

Rarely do couples agree 100 percent on anything, so humble compromise is the bedrock of healthy relationships. Minimalism is no different. To this day, my wife and I still disagree on things related to minimalism. Our two most common areas of disagreement seem to be clothing and children's stuff. But we have learned to work together in the areas where we do agree to keep our home clutter-free. So can you and your partner.

If you have kids, one of the most important steps you can take next is to agree together on how to introduce minimalism into their lives. As with other areas of parenting, it's important to present a unified front when persuading your kids to become part of the mini-mizing of your family lifestyle. So let this become a part of your conversation with your spouse.

I want to talk about minimalism with younger children before addressing the special issues involved with teenagers. But with both age ranges, there's something you always have to keep in mind.

Live it before you demand it.

If you want your children to buy less stuff, then you buy less. If you want them to donate their unneeded possessions, then you do the same—first.

Why should a child give up a toy if you're buying a boat that you'll take to the lake only twice a year?

Why should a child sort through her clothes to give away what she's outgrown if your own closet is stuffed to overflowing?

By having your spouse on your side working toward minimalism, the two of you together can present this lifestyle as a credible and achievable goal to your children, without inspiring their resentment.

MUNCHKIN MINIMALISTS

When Kim and I began minimizing, our kids were five and two. Today, they are thirteen and ten. I have seen them grow and mature in a home with less stuff than most of their neighborhood friends have. They're comfortable with our family lifestyle, and they are flourishing. They don't feel deprived at all. On the contrary, their lives are rich, as they are well on their way to becoming young adults of imagination, ambition, and originality.

Kim and I have made some mistakes (as all parents do), but we have also learned some important lessons along the way. By far, the most important lesson we have learned is this: It may be more difficult to become minimalist with kids, but it is also more important. Children who do not learn to set boundaries for themselves too often become adults who do not set boundaries for themselves.

But how, in a practical sense, do we help our kids navigate this process?

It differs between younger kids and older kids. With both age groups, you need to expect to do some educating, just as you do in negotiating minimalism with a spouse who is new to the subject. From that point, you can be more directive with younger kids and more persuasive with teens.

Your young children have probably never heard of minimalism, much less thought about it. So begin by describing minimalism in simple terms. Explain why you and your spouse are choosing to embrace a lifestyle of less as well as the benefits you are hoping your family will receive from it. Kids are often much smarter than we give them credit for. Yours will soon realize that you're not punishing them; you're doing this because you love them.

Listen to your children's questions and concerns, then provide answers as best you can. Assure them that your decision does not mean you are no longer going to buy anything. It just means you are going to think more carefully about your purchases in the future. Also, you are going to find some ways to get rid of things the kids no longer need.

Once your kids understand the goal and are at least partially willing to go along on this journey, work with them to identify items they own that would be easiest to eliminate. For example, you can begin by removing the clothes they no longer wear, the toys they no longer play with, the books they no longer read, and the craft supplies they no longer use. They'll find they can live without this surplus just fine.

As a result, they may begin to start asking themselves, *How much of this other stuff do I really need?* You might be surprised by how quickly your younger kids take to the new approach and how creative and assertive they can be in reducing possessions. Soon you might have some little minimalists on your hands.

To empower your kids in the process of minimizing and to encourage a more clutter-free environment in the future, establish boundaries—clear guidelines about what is okay to buy or to keep and what is not okay. For example, we have agreed with our daughter that she can keep as many toys as she wants as long as they fit in her closet. She can also keep as many art projects as fit in the clear plastic bin under her bed. Once her collections begin to exceed the boundaries (as they inevitably do), we will allow her to make the decisions about what to keep and what to remove. In our home, these conversations happen about twice per year.

Boundaries are powerful things for all of us, but they are especially powerful for young children, who tend to think in concrete terms. Boundaries will help them recognize the finite nature of money, space, and time. Boundaries will help them know what to do and what to expect. As a parent, use boundaries to your advantage, and praise your children whenever they are learning how to implement them effectively.

One way to celebrate progress in keeping to boundaries is to re-ward your children with fun experiences. If you have already been minimizing yourself (as you should—remember the importance of providing an example), then you should have some extra savings and the time to do something with it. Use these to create fun family expe-riences. Take a trip to the beach, enjoy a day at an amusement park, or go on a weekend jaunt to a nearby city. You don't need to spend all of your newfound savings on one trip, especially if you are trying to get out of debt, but creating an experience that highlights the benefits of your minimalism can go a long way in helping your children under-stand your decision and cement their participation.

The Problem with Turning Your House into a Toy Store

"I just don't know what to do, Joshua. She never seems happy." This statement by my friend Santiago grabbed my attention, and I sat up straighter in my chair.

Santiago is a few years older than I am and, financially speaking, more successful in every way: more income, more cars, bigger house, more toys. We were enjoying some wonderful food at a downtown restaurant and talking about marriage and parenting. At some point, our conversation turned to his elementary-age daughter.

My friend's face was showing frustration. "I don't understand. She has a whole drawer full of video games, a bedroom full of dolls, and a whole entire room in our house completely dedicated to toys. But she never seems happy. She is constantly telling me she's bored."

His attention began to shift. As is so often the case when it comes to parenting, he began thinking about his own childhood.

"When I was young," he said, "my family didn't have anything. I mean, Joshua, we were super poor. I only had three toys to play with, and I shared them with my three brothers. But we made do with what we had—and we had lots of fun. I don't ever remember asking my parents to buy me stuff."

I was ready with my response to this. I had spent years thinking about this topic and had just finished writing my book *Clutterfree with Kids*.

"Maybe your daughter is discontent because she has too *many* toys," I told Santiago. "Think about it this way. When you were young, you only had three toys. But more importantly, you knew that wasn't going to change. You had three, that's it. So you were forced to make do with what you had and find happiness in it. That was your only choice."

My friend was nodding, so I knew he was with me so far.

I went on: "Your daughter, on the other hand, is in a completely different circumstance. Whenever she wants something new, whether it's something she saw in a commercial or something her friend has, she just asks for it and then she gets it. You allow her to keep looking for happiness in the next toy, the next game, the next purchase. Heck, you practically encourage it. Maybe if she was forced to find happiness in the toys she already has, she just might find it. But for now, she is able to live under the impression that the next toy is going to bring it."

My friend's face grew sadder because he knew that what I was saying was true. His own decisions were contributing greatly to the unhealthy relationship his daughter had formed with possessions.

This is a reminder all of us parents need: Our kids need boundaries! If we don't give them a sense of how much is too much, they'll just keep wanting more. And if we let them grow up without considering the downsides of overaccumulation, we could be dooming them to repeat the errors of excess that are so common in our world today.

Don't you want to spare your kids the bondage that comes with having too much stuff? Start early to teach them that less is more—more fun, that is! It's one of the best ways you can show them your love.

BEFORE THE NEST EMPTIES

In my experience, it's often relatively easy to divert younger children onto a path of minimalism. I can't say the same thing about teenagers. They're more apt to resist. Yet helping them establish habits of living more simply is a crucial goal for the few remaining years you still have them at home.

I have worked with teenagers at churches in Nebraska, Wisconsin, Vermont, and Arizona, and I know them well. I can understand the reasons why they may resist the minimalist message. Teenagers seek out acceptance through conformity with their peers. Advertisers intentionally target the young adult demographic, hoping to influence their spending habits for life. Also, teenagers are beginning to exercise their own decision making more fully. They are less likely to value input from adults, especially parents.

If you parent teenagers, you know the challenges are formidable. But you should also recognize the benefits of reaching students with the message of minimalism. Many of their most significant decisions are still ahead of them. Because they have not started using credit, they are not held captive under the weight of creditors (hopefully things can stay that way!). While their spending habits are being shaped by any number of external factors, they are still not fully determined.

Not long ago, I pulled together a group of parents, mentors, and community leaders that I respect to share some wisdom on how to raise minimalist teenagers in an age of excess. I knew the collective wisdom would be incredibly valuable. Here are some of their thoughts:

- *Encourage idealism.* Many teenagers desire to find a cause that can change the world. But far too often grown-ups misunderstand and even discourage teenage idealism. We ought to encourage it! By describing the possibilities offered by minimalism, we can help our older children dream bigger dreams than simply aspiring to have the latest devices, cool cars, and someday a big house.

- *Require teenagers to pay for expensive items themselves.* All parents ought to provide food, clothing, shelter, and other basic necessities. And—within reason—all parents should give gifts to their kids. But asking your teenagers to purchase expensive items with their own money will create in them a stronger sense of ownership and a better understanding of the relationship between work and satisfaction.

- *Encourage teenagers to recognize the underlying messages in advertising.* Advertisements are not going away and we can never completely avoid them. Help your child read behind the marketing message by asking, "What are they really trying to sell you with this advertisement? Do you think that product will deliver on its promise?"

- *Find an ally.* By the time your children have reached the teenage years, your role as a parent has changed significantly. In most families, teenagers are beginning to express independence in their relationships with their parents. But that doesn't mean they'll never listen to an adult. Find someone in your community (perhaps a coach, a mentor, or a leader at your church) who supports your values, then provide opportunities for him or her to speak into your teenager's life.

- *Discourage entitlement in your family.* Often, as parents, we work hard to ensure a significant advantage for our children by providing for them at all costs. But as we do, we equally run the risk of not preparing them for life by neglecting to teach them the truths of responsibility. It is hard work maintaining our possessions—lawns have to be mowed, cars cleaned and maintained, laundry sorted, rooms tidied. Expose teenagers to this truth often. (Hint: chores.)

- *Travel to less developed countries.* I've taken a lot of teens on trips to poor areas of the world, and every one of them has been impacted by the disparity between what we own and what others own. Furthermore, the teens are almost always impressed by how happy other people seem to be despite owning so little. If you open your teen's eyes to

living conditions in the Third World, it will make the
First World's emphasis on consumerism begin to appear
foolish and misplaced. If you know of any local organizations or church groups leading this kind of trip, consider
trying to interest your teenager in it.

- *Teach them that what matters most is not what they
  own but who they are.* A noble character is a far more
  valuable asset than material goods. Believe this truth.
  Live out the implications of it yourself. And remind
  the teenagers in your life about it whenever a teachable
  moment arises.

In all of this, be patient and be persistent with your teens. The
older your kids are, the more difficult the transition to minimalism is
likely to be. After all, if you are like me, it took you thirty years to finally adopt a lifestyle of living with less. It would be foolish to assume
that your teens will adopt it in thirty minutes—or even thirty days.
But in time, you may see your older kids, like your younger ones,
learn to love the freeing potentials of minimalism. At the very least,
they will have your example and teaching to turn to in later days when
they need them most.

STUDENT MINIMALIST

Jessica Dang was a fifteen-year-old girl living in England with her
parents when she started reading books on Buddhism that described
principles of minimalism. "I was hooked right away," she told me. "It
appealed to me because it just made so much sense. Everybody wants

to be happy, and you don't need material possessions to be happy, even though most people think you do."

At the same time that Jessica was developing an attraction to minimalism, however, her parents were making more money than ever—and spending it too. Jessica recalled, "We got a bigger house, more clothes, a new car, shiny gadgets, and everything else people usually acquire as they gain wealth. It didn't get to ridiculous proportions, but a lot of the things we spent money on just ended up sitting around the house and gathering dust. One particular regret I have is helping my father buy a huge exercise machine, which we never ended up using! The house got more and more crowded, and as the rooms seemed to get smaller, it made me feel anxious to be at home and be surrounded by it all."

I asked Jessica how her teenage friends reacted to her minimalism.

She said, "Sometimes I felt that my friends and I were living in two different worlds. They worried about so many things, like the latest fashion, that I couldn't care less about. At the beginning I tried to say something about how they should relax a bit and not care about such material things, and that there were more important things in life. But it fell on deaf ears, and in the end I learned to keep quiet about it. I was preaching to the wrong crowd."

So instead Jessica started a blog called *Minimal Student,* where she wrote about her thoughts and experiments in minimalism.[1] There she found an online community of other young people who believed in the same things she did.

When it was time for college, Jessica packed everything she

needed in the trunk of her car and moved to another city. She loved being free to live simply and found that it was true that she really didn't need much to get by.

After only one year of college, she reduced her possessions to a single suitcase and moved to Japan for a year. "I had the most amazing year of my life," she said. "I did, saw, and tasted so many new and exciting things, and didn't even own my own weight in possessions. I didn't need it! After that year, my life was never the same. When I came back to England to finish my studies, I got my own place again and moved in with my few possessions. Those were the happiest years of my life."

Can you imagine Jessica ever becoming a big spender and over-accumulator? I can't. She's found a better way and it's going to stick for life. And minimalism took root within her when she was only a teen.

KEEPING THE RELATIONSHIP NUMBER ONE

Families everywhere have chased happiness in the form of riches and possessions for far too long. It is time we raise a generation that chooses to look elsewhere for the good life. And let me assure you again: minimalism as a family is completely achievable. My own family and many others I have known are proof.

Learn about minimalism. Talk about it. Model it. Set boundaries to establish it. Reap the benefits.

Own less as a family—you'll love it!

And now, before I conclude this chapter, I must put things in perspective for you with a reminder about something I hope you already understand: your relationships with your spouse and children matter so much more than where you are on the road to minimalism.

I have heard from a number of people who have taken steps toward minimalism in their lives but in the process have become so frustrated with their spouses or children that they have allowed strife and resentment to set in. Even worse, in a few cases, a one-sided pursuit of minimalism has driven families apart.

Once I received an e-mail that horrified me.

> Joshua, I would like your advice about something. I feel like I'm literally suffocating under all the stuff we own. My husband won't listen to me or consider parting with any of it. Do you think I should get a divorce?

As quickly as I could, I wrote back. A part of what I said was this:

> I can understand why you're feeling suffocated, but I definitely DON'T advise you to get a divorce. Minimalism should bring people closer together, not drive wedges between them.

What a mistake this woman was about to make!

Refuse to make a similar mistake yourself. Don't let issues about your stuff separate members of your family, whether legally or emotionally.

Remember, you chose minimalism for a reason. Most likely, you chose it at least in part because you valued relationships more than your possessions. If that is the case, then it would be foolish to allow minimalism itself to come between you and your loved ones. Your treasured relationships are just too important.

Realize that you can't change someone else. You can only educate, encourage, and assist, as permitted. You may not be fully satisfied with the response you get to minimalism from your family members. If that's the case, tell yourself that semi-minimalism is better than no minimalism at all. And if you made a vow to your partner that you would remain committed until death do you part, remain faithful to your word.

One of the greatest marks of love is patience. When you feel your frustration growing and you are ready to lash out in anger at one of your family members, take a deep breath. Remind yourself that you are not perfect either. In your mind, start a running list of all the good things you appreciate about your spouse and kids. Again, you can't change another person; you can only change your next interaction.

Now, it is possible that a family member's refusal to minimize her possessions may be symptomatic of deeper issues. Deep heart wounds may be causing your partner or child to be a hoarder. This person's behavior may even be a symptom of obsessive-compulsive disorder or another medical condition. In such a case, the correct approach is to tread lightly and find your family member the support and help that he needs. Sometimes this means professional help.

By all means, do your best to spread the minimalist message

within your family. There's nothing like knowing that your loved ones are right there beside you, pursuing changes that mean a lot to you. But whatever happens, keep your priorities straight.

Don't love things (or even the absence of things). Love people. Especially those who are closest to you.

And now that we've learned the steps of minimizing, including bringing our families along with us, it's time to focus on the bigger issues—the payoffs of minimizing. Remember, it's not just that our excessive possessions are not making us happy. What's worse, they are taking us away from the things that do. Once we let go of the things that don't matter, we are free to pursue all the things that really do matter.

Next, we're going to be looking at becoming more generous people (chapter 11), living intentional lives in every respect (chapter 12), and dreaming big dreams for our lives (chapter 13).

11

Shortcut to Significance

One day my family and I went grocery shopping and then left the store, only to find a large scratch along the side of our maroon mini-van where another car had scraped it. I immediately felt a sinking sensation in the pit of my stomach. Such an ugly mark, and so obvious to anyone who glanced at the passenger side of our van!

Worse than the scratch itself was the fact that the driver who had left it there had departed the scene without leaving his or her contact information so that we could access this person's insurance for the repair. This meant that if we were going to get the scratch fixed, we would have to pay for it ourselves. More likely, though, given the advanced age of the car, the scratch would remain there, spoiling its appearance.

My wife and I drove away in silence, both fuming.

In the quiet, I began to reflect on how the incident had impacted me. Why was I so upset about a scratch on our minivan?

I decided it was because our vehicle was such a large investment for us. It had cost us a lot of hard-earned money to buy this car, and we had spent a lot of time and energy caring for it. If I'd gotten a similar scratch on my bicycle, I wouldn't have been nearly so concerned. But because the car represented a major financial investment for us (our second largest, after our house), I had a lot of emotions invested in it too.

And then I remembered something Jesus said: "Where your treasure is, there your heart will be also."[1] Notice the order of his phrasing: our hearts follow our treasure, not the other way around.

Unfortunately, too many of us are tying our hearts to the wrong things. We are devoting our lives to material possessions that will never bring lasting joy. We shop for bigger houses, faster cars, trendier clothing, and cooler technology, and we shove more and more stuff into our already-packed closets. Subsequently, our clutter requires us to invest more and more time and energy into caring for it.

But lasting fulfillment can never be found in things that are temporal by nature. And our discontent is evidenced in our excess.

Instead, it is important for each of us to look outside ourselves—to find investments that tie our hearts to things that bring real joy, eternal purpose, and lasting fulfillment. I'm talking about our family, our friends, our spirituality, and the causes we believe in. Here is where we should be devoting more of our time, energy, and financial resources.

Living with less enables us to be more generous and giving. In fact, I've seen over and over again that minimalism can be the quickest shortcut to a life of greater and more lasting significance. A lot of people might want to be more generous, but until they free themselves from the burden of spending too much money and accumulating too many possessions, they will not be able to do it. There's a richness in turning our excess into someone else's supply. And the sooner we give to others, the sooner we discover the great potential each of our lives can hold.

Generosity, then, is not just an outcome of minimalism. It can also be a motivation for it.

Wouldn't you like to be making a difference for the better in the lives of others both near at hand and around the world? In this chapter I'm going to say to you: Give away some of your unneeded things, extra money, and available time. The benefits for both you and those you give to will be amazing.

GARAGE-SALE DUD

When Kim and I started minimizing, we were faced with the question of what to do with all the stuff we were getting rid of. Our goal at first was to get as much financial return as possible from the things we were discarding. My thinking ran like this: *I paid good money to buy these things, and I should get something in return.*

With that goal in mind, we tried different strategies. We posted items for sale on Craigslist. We took clothes to a consignment shop. We opened an account on eBay. (At one point, I placed my entire junk drawer on auction. Surprisingly, no bids!)

And of course we held a garage sale.

We decided to stage our sale one Saturday morning just weeks after we were introduced to minimalism. We woke early and rushed through breakfast, then got started working. We set up tables and placed dishware, clothes, toys, decorations, books, CDs, and DVDs (just to name a few of the items) where buyers could easily browse through the selection. We put a handwritten price sticker on each.

When everything was ready, we put up balloons by the street. We prayed that the rain would hold off. We played soft music, just as they do in department stores. And then we opened the doors for our big garage sale.

As we waited for customers, my wife and I talked about what we would do with the large sum of money we were expecting to receive. Put it in savings? Take a family trip? Maybe order new carpet for the living room? It seemed the possibilities were endless . . . until the reality set in.

While I sat on a green plastic chair, customers slowly came and went. They'd pick up items, turn them around to look at them, and then put them back. Kim and I chitchatted and made eye contact with as many customers as possible, hoping to make the buying experience friendly. Some folks were interested in some of the items, but often, in order to make a sale, we had to haggle over the price.

As the sun drifted across the sky and the afternoon came, we marked down some prices. We worked every angle to score more sales. At one point I even pretended to be a customer at my own sale just so drivers passing by would give our sale a second thought.

By the end of the day, we had earned $135. It was disheartening. We'd pocketed so much less cash than we had originally expected. We were depressed too. Let me tell you, there are few experiences in life that make you question your taste in home furnishings more than watching some of your favorite decorations not sell despite being marked down to twenty-five cents.

That night, too tired to even think about cooking, we spent half of our day's haul just taking the family out for dinner. Some financial move that garage sale turned out to be!

As a result of my experience on that summer day as well as similar experiences I've seen repeated many times, I have some advice for you: If you're getting rid of things to simplify your lifestyle, don't try selling them. It's not worth the trouble. Selling everything brings extra burden and stress to the minimizing process. Well, for some big-ticket items, selling might be worth the trouble. But not for all the little stuff—certainly not if you're depending on a garage sale to rake in big bucks!

Fortunately, we immediately found a different way.

THE BETTER WAY TO GET RID OF YOUR STUFF

After our disappointing, tiring, and time-wasting garage sale, Kim and I still had a lot of leftover items that we had to do something with. So Kim made a call to Care Net, a local organization in Burlington, Vermont, that supplied expectant mothers with maternity and baby wear. Kim wondered if they might be able to use some of the baby supplies we hadn't sold.

They responded enthusiastically. "Yes, yes we can. We always have a need."

Because of their response, I made another phone call. This time, I reached out to the Vermont Refugee Resettlement Program, which helps refugees and immigrants gain personal independence and economic self-sufficiency.

They explained to us that they had a desperate need for towels, linens, and cookware since they routinely outfit apartments for immigrants who arrive with little more than the clothes on their backs.

After this, we called more local charities, including a homeless shelter.

Our hearts were softened as we began to comprehend the number of men, women, and children in our community who live without the basic security that our household items could provide. In fact, to our chagrin, we realized that for years we had let some items that were desperately needed by others gather dust in our closets or basement. And for what reason? Just in case our supply of linens, cookware, or clothing suddenly proved to be inadequate?

We quickly discovered more joy in delivering those unneeded items to local charities than we could ever have found in the money earned from selling them. This experience changed my view of minimizing and forever changed my advice to others embarking on the journey.

Rather than sell your unwanted items, give them away. Practice generosity with them. There's no lack of opportunity.

Countless charitable organizations around the world meet real and urgent needs. They provide food and shelter to those without. They deliver clean water to villages lacking a well. They protect battered women. They place orphans in loving families. They offer educational assistance and job training to people who need help getting a start. And much, much more.

By giving your unneeded possessions to such organizations, you can make a real difference quickly and easily. And by getting a tax-deductible receipt, you can probably come out financially ahead of where you would have if you had sold items on eBay or at a garage sale—with much less effort! Certainly, the satisfaction you'll feel is like nothing else you experience, even if your garage sale brought in receipts exceeding your highest hopes.

Minimizing your possessions is hard work. Trying to resell your clutter only adds time and energy costs, as well as anxiety and frustration, to the journey. But giving away things adds joy and fulfillment to your soul that money can never buy.

So find a local charity whose values align with yours, and experience the delight of seeing how your excess can meet the needs of others in your community.

Ali Eastburn experienced this reality in a way that few others have ever considered.

WITH THIS RING

In 2007, Ali was a forty-year-old wife and mother with red hair and a sparkling personality when she attended a weekend retreat with some of the women from her church. She was expecting to reconnect with her friends and focus on her relationship with God. Little did she know this retreat would change her life and, eventually, the lives of numerous men and women all over the world.

As the women sat together in a room, the retreat leader asked, "What can we do to change the world around us?"

The room fell silent.

Finally Ali spoke up. "What if we sold some of our stuff and used the money to help people?"

Her idea was met with more silence. But Ali wasn't finished yet.

"What if we sold some of the stuff we love? Like a car or a boat or—" Ali broke off because a subversive thought had come into her mind, an idea that would change her life and the lives of countless others. She said, "I bet if I sold my wedding ring I could feed an entire village in Africa."

She couldn't believe the words coming out of her mouth. And yet she knew deep down that giving up her ring was exactly what she needed to do.

Weeks later, after more than one conversation with her husband, they sold the ring and donated the money to drill water wells in sub-Saharan Africa, where many were perishing for lack of clean drinking water.

But the story didn't end there. A few weeks later, one of Ali's friends pulled her aside on a Sunday morning and placed her wedding ring in Ali's hand. She said quietly, "You can have my ring too." To Ali's great surprise, it didn't stop there. Another friend gave up her ring. And then another.

Riding the momentum, Ali established a nonprofit organization called With This Ring that calls men and women into radical generosity, boldly asking them to part with their most prized possessions for the sake of others. To date, With This Ring has collected over a thousand rings and has provided clean water for tens of thousands of people in Africa, Central America, and India.[2]

Ali has experienced joy in giving and fulfillment in generosity. Indeed, she would attest that it is far better to give than to accumulate.

You may never feel moved to give up your wedding ring for the sake of providing clean water to people in Africa. Ali would be the first to admit that hers was a rare first step toward generosity. But each of us should feel moved to care for the poor and the needy, not just for their sake but for ours as well. Giving away our possessions offers an immediate way to start helping the most vulnerable around us.

And I'm just getting started in telling you how minimalism can empower your generosity.

INVESTING YOUR FINANCIAL DIVIDEND

Once we have made some progress in minimizing our lifestyle, an obvious benefit emerges. Because we have stopped buying so much stuff, we usually wind up with more money in the bank. I think of this money as the financial dividend of minimalism.

There are many things we can do with this dividend, such as pay off debt, save or invest for a more financially secure future, and buy quality over quantity when genuine needs arise. These are all good choices. But another one is to initiate or increase our charitable giving.

Take a guess as to what percentage of their income Americans give away each year.

The correct answer is that Americans as individuals, on average, give away somewhere between 2 and 3 percent of their income. That adds up to roughly $260 billion per year for the nation. If you add in the money contributed by foundations, corporations, and bequests, the total climbs to somewhere around $360 billion.[3]

Don't get me wrong; I am glad to see that money flowing to people who need it. Yet, I'll be honest with you, I think this is a paltry and even embarrassing amount. If we give away 3 percent as individuals, that means we keep 97 percent of our income for ourselves. With Americans among the wealthiest people on the planet, do we really need to spend 97 percent of our money on ourselves? Especially considering the great need all around the world and in our backyards?

I know it can be scary to give away money, especially if we haven't done much of that in the past. Generosity is an act of bravery. There's something hard about opening our hands and letting our hard-earned cash go. Just as we think we ought to hang on to our possessions "just in case," so we also think we need to hold on to as much money as we can "just in case."

Rarely, though, do we need to hold as much money in reserve as our panic would tell us we should. In fact, by reducing our expenses, minimalism reduces our financial risk.

So my advice about your excess money is to let it go. Be free with it. Learn to let it become a part of the great flow of financial value that travels toward people who need it.

You might be surprised by how good it feels.

You might also be surprised by how engaged in the whole process of generosity you become. Put your treasure someplace good, and your heart will follow.

Take the effort you used to put into researching your buying options and shopping for stuff you didn't really need, then use it instead to figure out how to give your money away with maximum impact. There is plenty of information out there that can turn you into an everyday philanthropist. In case this is a new endeavor for you, I want to give you some starter advice.

GROWING YOUR GIVING

Few of us are satisfied with our current level of generosity. Most people I know wish they were able to give more.

Because of that, I want to include a number of simple steps we can take to make generosity more intentional in our lives. If you have never given away any money, this would be a great way to get started (no matter what your current economic situation is). On the other hand, if you are hoping to raise the level of generosity in your life, you will also find some of these simple steps to be relevant and helpful.

1. *Start small—really small.* If you've never given away money, start by giving away $1. If you are embarrassed to give just $1, don't be. You've got nothing to worry about: there are plenty of charities online that allow you to give with your credit card, and you'll never cross paths with the people who record your $1 donation.

    Of course, the point of this exercise is not to report a $1 deduction on your year-end tax return. The point is to get started. If you'll feel more comfortable giving $5, $10, or $20, start there. But no matter what dollar amount you choose, get off the sideline and into the game with something. You can afford it. And that little push can help build momentum in your life toward fiscal generosity.

2. *Give first.* When you receive your next paycheck, make your first expense an act of giving.

    Often we wait to see how much we have left over

before we determine how much we can give away. The problem is that most of the time, after we start spending, there is nothing left over—and there are always more expenses looming in the future. The habit of spending all of it is too deeply ingrained in our lives. To counteract that cycle, we should give first.

Every payday, write a check to your church, a local homeless shelter, or whatever recipient you choose. You may be surprised by how you won't even miss it. You may also be surprised by how easy it will be to increase your gift over time.

3. *Divert one specific expense.* For a set period of time, divert one specific expense to a charity of your choosing. You may choose to bring a lunch to work instead of going to a restaurant, ride your bike to work once a week instead of burning fuel to drive your car, or give up Starbucks on Mondays (wait—make that Thursdays). Calculate the money you'll save, then redirect it to a specific charity or cause.

I recommend picking something that would be fun to give up, something unique that you'll remember. Setting a specific period of time for the experiment should make it completely achievable for you.

4. *Fund a cause based on your passions.* There are countless charities and causes that need your support. And some of them are directly in line with your most compelling passions.

What are you most passionate about? Is it the
environment, poverty, or religion? Maybe it's world
peace, child nutrition, or animal rights. What about
education, civil rights, or clean water? Identify what
passions already move you, find a committed organization working in that area, and then joyfully help them
in their work.

5. *Spend time with a generous person.* Once, I found
myself out to lunch with an older gentleman whose
generosity I had admired for years and decided to ask
questions about the practice in his life. I started with
"Have you always been such a generous guy?" When he
answered, "No, I haven't been," I immediately followed
with more: "When did you become so generous?"
"How did it start?" "How do you decide where your
money goes?" "What advice would you give to someone
who wants to get started?" The conversation was
helpful to me as I began to lay a foundation for my own
practice of generosity. (And the other guy paid for the
meal. Go figure.)

Generosity rarely happens by chance. Instead, it is an intentional
decision each of us must make with our lives. But it does not need to
be as difficult as many people think. Sometimes, starting with the
simple steps is the most important move we can take.

One big part of the more of less is that you can grow in
generosity.

INVESTING YOUR TIME DIVIDEND

When it comes to finding ways to be generous, think beyond the possessions you can donate.

Think beyond your cash too.

Think about you.

Minimalism typically yields not only a financial dividend but also a time dividend. When you've decided to purposely live with less, you're not so busy earning money to buy stuff, buying the stuff, and then taking care of the stuff you bought. So you've got more time for other things. Consider using some of that time to get directly and personally involved in good works by volunteering.

I know this step can be scarier than dropping off a donation or writing a check. It's more personal, more vulnerable. It will mean that you actually get involved with people, and that always has the potential to be messy. But what I like best about volunteering is that it reminds me that people with needs are people and not projects. And I know that every time I have taken the risk to give of my time, my energy, and my abilities, I have been glad I did it.

I believe there is a ladder of impact in generosity. Donating possessions is good. Giving money is usually even better. But the best by far is getting personally involved in serving others.

Afraid that you don't have anything to offer? I believe you do! You have your strength. You have your compassion. You have your wisdom from lessons learned. You may have an administrative knack, a creative bent, a building skill, or any number of other gifts you can share with people and organizations.

When you think about volunteering, assess your gifts as well as your passions. Match these with the needs you can find. Do you see yourself organizing a canned-foods drive? Walking dogs at an animal shelter? Serving as a docent at a historical site? Tutoring literacy? Building a home for a poor family?

Plenty of organizations are available to plug in with. Consider your faith congregation. A homeless shelter. A food bank. A library. A hospital. A senior-citizens center. An environmental organization. A national park. An art museum. A school.

Once you become an old hand at volunteering, maybe you'll be ready to go further afield. Maybe you'll offer disaster relief with the Red Cross. Or join a missions team. Or sign up with the Peace Corps.

But before the possibilities start to sound intimidating, let me remind you that volunteering doesn't need to be nearly as formal and organized as any of that. All it really takes is having a heart of love for others, eyes to see what they're going through, and time to come alongside them. You can make life better for others simply by shoveling the snow from the driveway of an elderly neighbor, baby-sitting kids to give respite to a weary mom, or making meals for a sick friend. Simple acts of compassion like these make the world a kinder, less lonely place.

Generous people are quick to admit that one person will never solve all the world's ills. But that does not slow them one bit. To them, the possibility of changing even one life for the better is enough to be getting on with.

As Anne Frank said, "How wonderful it is that no one has to wait, but can start right now to gradually change the world!"[4]

GENEROSITY'S BLOWBACK

Clearly, when we give away our unneeded stuff, our extra money, and our available time, we can make life better for others. But in a beautiful way, our generosity is good for us too.

I'm not saying that we should be generous *so that* we can benefit from it personally. We should be generous for the sake of others—that's our motivation. But at the same time, we should expect some intangible benefits to blow back to us, and we should accept them gratefully.

I can attest that generosity makes me feel better about myself and what I'm doing with my life. And I know I'm not alone. Many people who are generous report a greater sense of satisfaction and happiness. Studies have even linked generosity to improved physical health.[5] Amazing!

Furthermore, I've observed that generous people have more fulfilling relationships. People always enjoy the company of a generous giver to the company of a selfish hoarder. People are naturally attracted to others who have an open heart to share with others. And being a good friend is the best gift you could ever give yourself.

Those who are generous also tend to value what they own. People who give away possessions hold their remaining possessions in higher esteem. People who donate money are far less wasteful with the money left over. And people who give their time make better use of their remaining time.

Yet all the while, generous people find meaning outside their possessions. Although many people wrap up self-worth in net worth (as if a person's true value could ever be tallied on a balance sheet!), generous people find their value in helping others. They quickly realize that their bank statements say nothing about their true value.

Because of this, they have less desire for more. They have found fulfillment, meaning, value, and relationships outside the acquisition of possessions. They have learned to find joy in what they already possess and give away the rest. In other words, they have found contentment.

But maybe the greatest benefit of generosity is this: generous people realize that they already have enough.

Too often we are held hostage by the pursuit of more. No matter how much we have, we always seem to need more—more stuff and more money.

We choose our careers for the sake of securing more. We spend the best hours of our days trying to obtain more. We get jealous when "less deserving" people seem to have more. And we constantly worry about having enough.

But this constant desire for more is having damaging effects on our society. Seventy-two percent of us report feeling stress about money.[6] There are some who experience this anxiety because of legitimate financial need, but for most of us, this stress is completely misplaced. In a world where six billion people live on less than $13,000 per year, [7] most of our financial-related stress occurs because of artificially manufactured need.

Generosity changes these thoughts and helps to remove this pursuit. It reveals to us how blessed we already are. It reminds us we already own more than we need. It shows us how much we have to give and how much good we can accomplish. It helps us see the needs of those we live alongside. And it offers a better alternative for our money than spending it on ourselves.

If you're motivated by a desire to be more generous, let it spur you on to live with less. And as your minimizing frees up resources you can share, go ahead and give them away with freedom and joy. Your heart will feel warmer. The world will be a better place. And you will discover you never even needed the stuff in the first place.

So this very day, donate clothing you don't wear, sporting equipment you don't use, books you aren't going to read, or furniture needlessly taking up space. Make a financial donation to a charity you support. Be generous with your time by volunteering at your local school, a homeless shelter, or the nonprofit of your choice.

It's the quickest shortcut I can suggest to having a life of impact.

An Intentional Life

My life looks very different today than it did in 2008, and minimalism has been the catalyst. Deciding to own less has brought more changes to my life than simply cleaner drawers and closets. It has challenged many of my assumptions and prompted a whole new lifestyle.

Looking back now, I have the benefit of comparison.

I used to love watching television and playing hours of video games. I had an allergy to exercise, drank lots of soda, and ate too much fast food. I'd stay up late and sleep in whenever possible. I was doing all the things I thought I wanted to do.

But now I can see how my previous way of living was not improving my satisfaction. It was actually detracting from it. The life I was living wasn't even close to the best one possible, for me or for those closest to me. It was a life of drifting, not focused direction.

This is what makes the unexamined life so dangerous. We think we are living life to the fullest but we aren't. Instead, we are often trading long-term purpose for short-term pleasure.

When we eat unhealthily, we miss an opportunity to fuel our bodies properly.

When we watch too much TV or spend too much time online, we miss opportunities to interact with people in the real world.

When we neglect to exercise, we miss the opportunity to enjoy the kinds of adventures available to those with physical stamina.

When we stay up late and sleep through the morning, we may be missing out on the most productive period of our day.

When we buy more than we need, we miss the opportunity to live free and unburdened.

When we spend more than we earn, we shackle ourselves with bondage to debt.

When we spend too much money on ourselves, we miss the opportunity to find greater joy by being generous to others.

The way to avoid these kinds of mistakes is to live intentionally. That is, we examine our options and make choices with larger purposes and longer-term goals in mind. If an activity, a decision, or a habit is not bringing us closer to our purpose and passion, then we should remove it. Because most of the time it is only distracting us from what really matters.

Up to this point in the book, I have talked mostly about our possessions, since they have such a hold on us and because it is such a big project to right-size our material environment. But the principle of getting more out of less applies far beyond our household goods.

Let's consider three common areas where we can benefit by applying intentionality to our lives: our schedules, our bodies, and our relationships.

ADDICTED TO BUSYNESS

The speed of our world is ever increasing. Technology and communication continue to improve, and information moves faster. All the while, employers and social-media networks appear to reward those who remain perpetually connected.

Expectations, demands, and accessibility continue to expand, but the number of hours in a week does not. As a result, our lives only get busier and busier.

Statistics tell the tale. In Britain, 75 percent of parents are too busy to read to their children at night.[1] A rising number of children are being placed in day-care facilities and after-school activities.[2] We are having a hard time finding opportunities for vacations.[3] On average, Americans rate their stress level as a 4.9 on a 10-point scale, largely due to the busyness of their schedules and the pressure to make money to support the accepted lifestyle.[4]

Our fast-paced approach to life rarely benefits us in the long run, because a busy life is an unreflective life. Often we get so wrapped up in scurrying from one thing to another that we don't even realize how our schedules are overwhelming us. Nor do we recognize how our overcommitted lives may actually be harming us.

Seemingly, busyness has become the default state for too many of us. Just as we overspend and overaccumulate material possessions, so we overcommit our calendars.

Certainly there are seasons in life that require focused time and commitment. And we should never discourage working hard on things that matter. Unfortunately, however, most of us have become busy over all the wrong things and we have allowed false assumptions to drive our schedules.

Many of the lies we have been told since birth crowd out the things in life that matter most. Instead of enjoying the benefit of calm, intentional living, we hurry from one needless triviality to another. And in the end, nobody wins.

Don't get so busy chasing the wrong things that you miss enjoying the right things.

BECOMING UNBUSY

My friend Mike Burns gives a testimony that it is possible to simplify your schedule and make life unbusy. He says,

Fifteen years ago, I was overwhelmed.

I was working a ton of hours, trying to establish myself in my career. I was juggling relationships with my wife, my six kids, neighbors, friends, family, and co-workers. My schedule was pretty cluttered. There was a lot of stuff going on, and not enough time to do it.

My intentions were good. My heart was in the right place. But my life was a whirlwind. I couldn't catch my breath.

Something had to change. I knew I needed some help.

So, my family began a journey to figure out how we could manage our time well and focus on the things that were most important to us. This pursuit has lasted fifteen years (and counting). And it has paid off tremendously!

I can't say that every day goes exactly according to plan. That's not even possible. But, I can say, with confidence, that we now live the kind of lives we want to live. We focus our efforts on those things we value most.[5]

If that sounds like the good news you want to be able to report about your life fifteen years from now, let me give you four steps to get there.

1. *Cultivate space in your daily routine.* Find space in your morning to sit quietly before starting your day. Take time for lunch. Make use of opportunities for breaks at work in between projects. Invest in solitude, prayer, or meditation. Begin right away to cultivate little moments of space and margin in your otherwise busy day.

2. *Reduce distractions.* These days, with a click of a mouse or swipe of a thumb, we are instantly transported into a world that will gladly absorb all our curiosity. Yet you cannot grow in one area of life if you are curious about all areas. Be intentional about limiting distractions by turning off smartphone notifications and apps, checking e-mail only twice a day, and reducing the number of times you log in to news, entertainment, and social media.

3. *Find freedom in the word no.* Seneca wrote, "Everybody agrees that no one pursuit can be successfully followed by a man who is busied with many things."[6] Recognize the inherent value in the word *no.* Learning to say no to less important commitments opens your life to pursue the most important.

4. *Appreciate and schedule rest.* One of the reasons many of us keep busy schedules is that we fail to recognize the value of rest. But rest is beneficial to our bodies, our minds, and our souls. Set aside one day per week for rest and family. Schedule it on your calendar and then guard it at all costs.

The principles of living with less apply to our schedules, calling us to remove the nonessential. They also bring intentionality to our health and body care.

SKIN DEEP

We live in a beauty-obsessed society. We might criticize this obsession at times, but still, most of us devote an incredible amount of time and energy to thinking about how we look, talking about how we look, and trying to look better to others. This is a major part of why so many of us lead cluttered, costly, and complicated lives.

Americans alone spend over $12 billion per year on plastic surgery and over $56 billion on cosmetics.[7] New diet fads surface and fade away at a dizzying pace. Magazine covers in grocery-store check-out aisles promise six-pack abs. The average woman spends two weeks per year on her appearance.[8]

By the way, it's not just women who tend to spend a lot of time trying to make themselves look good. The makers of men's grooming products are rubbing their hands in glee at trends indicating that men are becoming more focused on their looks. In fact, one survey carried out in the United Kingdom showed that men actually spent slightly more time than women in grooming.[9]

And then there is clothing. The average American family spends $1,700 per year on clothes.[10] Of course, we need some clothing, but we buy much of our clothing because we think it makes us look better to others or because it makes us feel better about ourselves. Today the average woman owns thirty outfits, whereas in 1930 she owned nine. She spends more than one hundred hours on thirty trips to shop for clothes, fifteen shoe-shopping excursions taking forty hours, and a full fifty hours per year window shopping.[11] Meanwhile, the average American throws away sixty-eight pounds of clothing per year.[12]

I won't do more than mention jewelry, hairdos, mani-pedis, skin treatments, and tattoos and piercings—all things that people pour time and money into in the pursuit of looking attractive.

The irony is, all this effort isn't necessarily showing the results we hope for. One survey showed that 77 percent of adult women still complain about their physical appearance, despite all the time and money spent.[13] Another research study revealed that on average, if women used 40 percent less makeup, both men and other women would find them more attractive.[14]

More importantly in the long run, despite all the cultural fixation on our bodies, we aren't nearly as healthy as we could be. Almost 69 percent of Americans are either overweight or obese.[15] Only one in five adults meets federal guidelines for both aerobic activity and muscle-strengthening exercise.[16] We spend $110 billion per year on fast food and average thirty-four hours per week watching television.[17] The problem here is that we are more focused on beauty than on health.

How much time and money are you spending on your looks? Perhaps more than necessary. If your closet is stuffed with clothes, your bathroom counter is crowded with beauty products, and you feel rushed every morning when getting ready for the day, and at the same time you know you're not as fit and strong as you could be, then maybe body care is an area where you can improve your life by becoming more intentional.

YOUR BODY, AN INSTRUMENT OF YOUR WILL

What perspective might motivate you to care for your body properly without becoming obsessive over it? I like what Gary Thomas, the author of *Every Body Matters,* says: we need to "stop treating our bodies like ornaments—with all the misguided motivations often displayed by those who build their bodies out of pride and ambition—and start treating our bodies like *instruments,* vessels set apart to serve the God who fashioned them." [18]

Appearance isn't what matters most. More importantly, our physical bodies are the instruments through which we accomplish our purpose in this world. Whether you or I desire to be a good parent, a spiritual mentor, a world traveler, a successful businessperson, or anything else, our bodies' condition is either an asset or a liability.

This implies that we need to make an important change in our thinking. We do not care for our bodies simply for vanity's sake or to fill an emotional void within us. We care for our bodies so we can more effectively accomplish what we most want to do with our lives.

This line of thinking drives us to make healthy choices:

- *It motivates us to fuel properly.* I am not a vegetarian, nor do I place strict restrictions on my diet, but I can recognize how healthy eating prepares me to live a more effective and efficient life. A good rule of thumb is to make half of your meal fruits and vegetables. The goal in our home is to make meat the side dish rather than the main dish.

- *It calls us to hydrate sufficiently.* Every system in your body depends on water. According to the Mayo Clinic, your body needs from nine to thirteen eight-ounce cups of fluid each day (depending on your gender, size, and activity level).[19] Consider eight glasses of water each day as a good place to start.

- *It invites us to exercise frequently.* The US Centers for Disease Control and Prevention recommends 150 minutes per week of aerobic and muscle-strengthening activities, performed on two or more days a week.[20] If you are intentional about getting exercise, you are meeting this suggestion. If you are not intentional about getting exercise, take a first step.

- *It requires us to eliminate unhealthy habits strategically.* I bet you don't even need me to repeat the common advice; you just need to follow it. Don't overeat. Eat less junk food. Drink less alcohol. Don't eat out as often. Don't smoke. Read and heed food labels.

The list I have provided above is not unique. What *is* unique is the motivation behind it. I don't adopt these principles out of envy or jealousy or from a need to impress people with my looks. I adopt these principles because they allow my body to more effectively accomplish my purpose in life. This mind-set shift makes a huge difference.

Pick one item from this list that you can improve upon. Start there. And experience some victories before moving on to the next.

HOW MINIMALISM LED TO A GYM MEMBERSHIP

Six months after discovering minimalism, I was faced with an upcoming birthday on December 11. My wife asked me what I wanted as a birthday present, and I didn't know how to answer. After spending months removing the clutter from our home, the last thing I wanted was to bring more stuff into our house. How could I ask for a tie when I had just donated twelve? Or another watch when I had just gotten rid of three?

Inspiration struck on a chilly evening while I was driving home from work. As I was passing a strip mall near our neighborhood, I saw a bright purple banner that hadn't been there before. It said, "Planet Fitness. Coming soon! Join now for only $10 per month."

Now I knew exactly what I wanted for my birthday: a gym membership. Not only would the gift result in zero new clutter added to our house, but also, for the first time, I had the time, the motivation, and the finances to get in shape and place a priority on conditioning my body.

On December 12, I paid my first visit to Planet Fitness. I've been exercising regularly and reaping the benefits of this new habit ever since.

In my case, minimalism spurred a change in how I treat my body, just as it caused me to simplify my schedule. Minimizing my possessions served as a gateway to intentionality in every other area.

This brings us to our third major area of intentionality when we want to live a lifestyle of less: relationships. Does the process of reducing and removing apply even here?

SAYING YOUR GOOD-BYES

A lot of people in the minimalism movement will advise, "Remove every person who does not bring benefit into your life." They're encouraging the elimination of relational clutter, just as they encourage us to clean the clutter out of our closets and off our shelves.

I understand the point they are trying to make, but I differ here. I believe it's a mistake to routinely apply the same filter to our relationships that we apply to our material goods. People are not the same as possessions. Relationships are not transactions. I'll have more to say about this soon.

But first I do want to acknowledge that there are times when it may make sense to let go of a relationship, and when we need to do it, we should do it effectively and without self-guilting. You might need to bring a relationship to an end if the relationship is harming you physically or emotionally, if neither of you is receiving any real benefit from it, or if putting time into this relationship is hindering a more important one.

Sometimes the best move is to cut off a relationship entirely. Abusive and codependent relationships, in particular, are prime candidates for removal, unless they can be fundamentally altered. Do the breakup kindly if you can, but do it.

In other cases you might just need to put limits or boundaries on a relationship. For example, you might decide, *I'll only talk with Mom on the phone once a week, except in emergencies.* Or you'll say to a friend, "I have to be honest with you, Tom—I don't want to hang out with you anymore unless you'll stop talking trash about your ex. It's just too toxic."

There are rhythms and balances and trade-offs that can make our relational lives healthier. Every good-bye makes room for a new hello. When you remove or reduce a harmful relationship, you'll experience less distraction and more peace. You'll have more time, more energy, and better emotional resources to devote to the people and things that matter most to you.

And do you know what? The chances are good that the person you have said good-bye to will be better off in the long run too!

Having said all that, let me repeat that the path to better living is not essentially found in turning our backs on others, even though it might occasionally be necessary for us to do so. The path to better living is found in developing the compassion and the space to love even those who don't deserve it. Choosing to invest only in the relationships that benefit us isn't love—it's selfishness.

VALUING A ONE-SIDED FRIENDSHIP

I have a friend. Let's call him John. Come to think of it, I'm not sure that *friend* is the best word to use for him, but it is the word I choose to use.

You see, John doesn't return many of my phone calls. He doesn't reply to my voice-mail messages. And he doesn't answer many of my texts.

But every few months, my phone will ring and John will be on the other end. Always out of the blue. Usually in the evening. He will apologize for having been gone so long. He will assure me that he is in a better place now, and he will ask if we can get together again for coffee or lunch.

If at all possible, I agree.

John's life has not been easy. He has told me of the abandonment, the drugs, the alcohol, and the homeless nights that define his past. He speaks freely of his indiscretions. His own failings are as much a part of his story as the home he grew up in.

Every time we get together, he shows up looking scruffy and unshaved but with a hopeful expression on his face. He will tell me about his desire to get back on the right track with God and about the recovery meetings he has been attending. I will assure him there are people cheering for him, and I will offer to help in any way I can. "Maybe we can get together again next week" is usually the last thing I say to him . . . until I hear from him again in a few months.

If I were to be honest, I would have to say that I'm not getting much out of my relationship with John. He doesn't offer me any advice. He doesn't have a job or a specific life skill that I can learn from. He certainly doesn't have any friends in high places who can help me get ahead. I think he cares about me as a person, but even if I'm right about that, he has a funny way of showing it.

The one thing that he does offer is frequent opportunities for me to give love. Not a love that expects something in return but a pure, unselfish love. One that requires patience and grace, commitment and sacrifice. You know—real love. Our relationship provides me the opportunity to remind him on a consistent basis that, no matter where he has wandered away to, I am patiently waiting for him to return.

There have been people over the years whom I have decided to gently disengage from. But there are also people, like John, whom I want to keep in my life despite the fact that my relationships with them don't score highly in a cost-benefit analysis.

The goal is not to remove every person from my life who does not serve me. The goal is to bring greater intentionality into each of my relationships. I want to find people who will lead me, mentor me, and love me, but I also want to keep in my life people whom I serve and love and pour my life into. Because both are required for a balanced life.

THOROUGHLY MINIMALIST

As minimalism becomes a part of who you are, you will find ways to live out its principles well beyond your material possessions. It will teach you to be intentional about what you say yes to and what you say no to in so many areas. We've looked at three of the major ones.

In your schedule . . . bring your busyness down to a healthy level, and focus on activities that matter the most to you.

In your body care . . . don't go overboard in trying to make yourself look good to others, but instead try to keep your body fit and capable for the purposes you hope to fulfill.

In your relationships . . . let go of unhealthy or unfruitful connections, if necessary, but keep up the ones that are important to you, even if sometimes the benefits to you aren't obvious.

Those who experience the greatest joy are the ones who seek to implement wise and healthy habits in all aspects of their being. Because when they do, they are equipped to accomplish more with their lives than they ever imagined.

And accomplishing things with our lives is what minimalism is all about. I've said it from the beginning: minimalism frees us up to pursue big dreams in our lives. To cap off the journey of *The More of Less,* that's exactly what we're going to look at next.

Don't Settle for Less

I set a goal for myself when I started writing this book: to introduce you to a lifestyle of owning less without ever letting you lose sight of the purpose for it—namely, finding freedom to pursue the things that matter most to you.

Have I succeeded? While reading, have you been thinking about the big dreams you have for your life? Or even better, have you started to experience the freedom of owning less and the fulfillment of living out some of those dreams?

I hope your home is beginning to look fresher, more peaceful, and more inviting. I hope you're no longer stumbling over stuff you don't need, wasting time trying to find a lost shoe in all the mess, or dreading coming home to a house that will only increase the stress you're already feeling. I hope your schedule, your self-care habits, and your relationships are less draining and more energizing. Review the preceding chapters of this book as often as you need to for inspiration or guidance in establishing and maintaining the minimalism that works best for you.

But if all we do is minimize our lifestyle without taking advantage of the dividends of time, money, and freedom that minimalism yields, then it would be like contributing regularly to a retirement investment account during your career and yet never spending the money on your retirement.

I talked in the previous chapter about intentionality. The most important type of intentionality lies in pursuing your greatest passions and most cherished dreams, now that minimalism has freed you up to do so.

So I can't finish this book without urging you in the clearest possible terms, *Go for it!* Book the airline tickets. Sign up for the art class. Call the volunteer coordinator. Train for the triathlon. Open the boutique. Take the pilot's lessons. Move closer to the grandkids. Record your songs. Climb the mountain. Learn French cooking. Write the novel. Finish the degree. Take in the foster children. Ride a horse in competition. Whatever it is you've dreamed about doing if you ever had the resources, do it now.

Somewhere in the world today minimalist Annette Gartland is living her dream of traveling the planet.

Somewhere in the world minimalist Dave Balthrop is doing the creative writing he loves.

Somewhere in the world I am still loving my new career of talking to people about the beauty of owning less.

You too will find your greatest possible life when you get out there and do whatever it is you are passionate about. Don't just dream a dream. Live it!

THE PEARL

One afternoon Jesus began talking to his followers about the value of the kingdom of heaven. As he so often did, he used a story to make his point, a story that would soon transcend religion and take up residence in world culture. The story went like this: "The kingdom of heaven is like a merchant looking for fine pearls. When he found one of great value, he went away and sold everything he had and bought it."[1]

I think we can safely imagine this merchant owned a lot of stuff before coming across the exceptional pearl. He probably thought his stash of goods was pretty nice too. But when he found something more valuable—the pearl—this merchant was wise enough to realize that, by comparison, his current possessions didn't measure up at all.

What I want to point out is that he didn't say "What a nice pearl" and then forget all about it. He didn't exaggerate the value of his current possessions in his mind or downplay the value of the special pearl. He wasn't lazy or timid, letting this opportunity slip by. Nor did he allow anybody to talk him out of his decision. No. He took decisive action to sell his current possessions and acquire the pearl.

Christians such as myself recognize that Jesus was drawing attention to the kingdom of God, urging his followers to forsake all in pursuit of it. But for our purposes here, I want to focus not on the identity of the pearl but on the actions of the merchant. He exemplifies for all of us wisdom in minimalism.

To look at this story a different way, then, minimalism is the process of "selling" our current possessions, and the "pearl" is whatever purpose minimalism allows us to pursue. You get to define this particular pearl for yourself. But whatever the pearl happens to be for you, take a cue from the merchant. Take action. Do what it takes to acquire the pearl. Don't allow any excuses to keep you from the better life available to those who choose to live with less.

As you're planning to do that, I want to offer some closing thoughts, both encouraging and challenging, about searching for the best possible pearl.

CONSIDER THIS

The story of the pearl of great price illustrates an important principle: life is about choices, but some choices are more valuable than others. Some things matter more. Some things matter less. There is greater life available for those who recognize the difference. And there are some endeavors worth sacrificing everything for.

This principle lies at the very foundation of minimalism. There are more valuable pursuits available to us than the purchase and accumulation of material possessions. And when we begin to recognize these opportunities, removing every distraction that's keeping us from them doesn't feel like sacrifice. It feels like the smartest thing we could do with our lives right now.

That's exactly the point where my minimalist journey began. When I was confronted with the realization that my physical possessions were taking me away from spending time with my five-year-old son, removing them became easier. I had identified a pearl, and giving up what it took to attain it was the only wise response.

This principle that some choices are inherently more valuable than others also applies to what you choose to do with the new freedom your minimalism provides. You can do anything you want, but you can't do everything. You can invest your minimalism "dividends" here or there, but not everywhere. So what's the best choice?

I have been saying all along that your greatest purpose is whatever you choose or however you define it. And that's true. You have the freedom. It's not my place to tell you what you should do with the resources minimalism will free up for you.

Still, I do want to make a special plea: Not only is your life too valuable to waste chasing material possessions, but it is also too valuable to waste pursuing only selfish interests with the freedom you have gained. Instead of pursuing only objectives that benefit you, make sure you are also doing good for others.

I suppose, after minimizing your possessions, you *could* move to a beachfront cottage and spend every day fishing. Or you *could* show up at the golf course day after day. And if something like that appeals to you, it's up to you. But I think you have a better choice available to you: improving the life of someone else.

How about mentoring new business owners for free with the knowledge you gained during your career?

Or starting a program to connect the homeless in your community with the public services that are available to them?

Or setting up a scholarship at your alma mater?

Or taking charge of a ministry team at your church?

Or organizing a group of doctors and dentists to provide free services in a region of the world that lacks medical and dental care?

Or letting your mom stay with you instead of living in the nursing home that makes her miserable?

Serving others is really a natural follow-up to minimalism, if you think about it. Minimalism in itself is an unselfish act, because it uses up fewer resources that others need. So investing the dividends of minimalism in the service of others is a logical extension of the same ethos of selflessness.

Of course it's not necessarily either/or. You can go fishing occasionally *and* lead a ministry team. You can still golf sometimes *and* mentor a new business owner.

But I'd hate to see you completely ignore options that put you in the position to help others. In fact, if in certain situations you have to choose between a more self-centered pursuit and a more others-centered one, I'd rather you choose the latter. Because it really is inherently more valuable.

There are many reasons why the biggest dreams are dreams that help others. Service does more than affect just us; it affects many other people as well. Helping the needy can have a multiplying effect if our actions inspire others to follow our example. It tends to bring people together rather than leave them in their own lanes in life. It reduces loneliness and fear, envy and resentment. It goes into a world that is too often dark and sad and brings light and joy.

And there's still one more reason why the biggest dreams are self-less dreams: because self-centered pleasure is never as rewarding in the long run as the satisfaction we feel in serving others.

THE PARADOX BEYOND THE PARADOX

This is a book about living with less so that you can get more out of your days. It's been about having a smaller material lifestyle so that you can experience a bigger life, full of passion and purpose. Own less to live more. That's paradoxical.

But there's another paradox that shows up when we begin to look at what, specifically, we will do with the money, time, and freedom that our minimalism has given us. Pursuing me-centered objectives can provide us with some happiness, but pursuing others-centered goals provides us with even better, more fulfilling happiness. It seems backward, but it's true.

I realize that some may believe this line of thinking is unrealistic, far-fetched, or old-fashioned. They believe that, in a dog-eat-dog world, if they're not looking out for number one, then nobody is. But it's their line of thinking that is shortsighted.

The reality—proven over and over again—is that people who serve others tend to have higher self-esteem, better psychological adjustment, and more happiness than those who don't. Their altruism improves their health and even extends their longevity. Their social connectedness improves, and everyone benefits: communities with significant citizen involvement are more stable and better places to live. Researchers cite a positive effect on grades, self-concept, and attitudes toward education among teens who volunteer. Service to others also leads to reduced drug use and huge declines in dropout rates and teen pregnancies. Choosing to help others consistently ranks as one of the most important ways to improve well-being.[2]

Before I hammer my point home too hard, let me affirm that I am not entirely against self-interest. The pursuit of happiness by doing what we enjoy or feel that we need for ourselves is not necessarily an unhealthy pursuit. It is important to feed our own souls, to enjoy recreation, and to care for ourselves effectively.

But when we try to find happiness in pursuits that *only* benefit us, we fall short of the truest and purest forms of happiness. Our pearl turns out to be counterfeit. So, as strange as it may seem, the most efficient pathway to lasting happiness and fulfillment is not to pursue them directly by serving ourselves but through helping others.

Consider what happens to us when we choose to serve others: life flips upside down. In helping others rather than seeking our own gain, we find greater freedom. We live lives of less stress, less anxiety, and less frustration. We begin to feel more fulfilled, more complete, more alive. Living for others abolishes our need for a pecking order. It lifts a great weight off our shoulders because we no longer seek power and mastery over others. We know what we're doing, and we know it matters. We have contentment and purpose.

What I've been saying in all this may be nothing new to you. In fact, your dreams for your future may already be filled with visions of ways you can serve others. If so, I'm thrilled about that! I imagine that's because you have already experienced the joy of serving, as I have, and it has whet your appetite for more of the same. In your case, minimalism will allow you to grow, refine, and fulfill your plans in ways you never imagined.

I want you to have a big dream. I also want you to get big-time satisfaction out of it. That will happen when your dream involves helping people besides yourself.

The Bengali poet Rabindranath Tagore wrote, "I slept and dreamt that life was joy. I awoke and saw that life was service. I acted and behold, service was joy." [3] Let me tell you about one way I "awoke" to find that life is service and service is joy.

THE HOPE EFFECT

When I received the advance payment for writing this book, my wife and I had an important decision to make. Because we have been living a minimalist lifestyle, we didn't need the advance to cover a burdensome mortgage payment, pay off a vehicle, get out of consumer debt, or buy new furniture for the living room. We didn't have to put it back into the business, into retirement, or into our kids' college fund. Minimalism provided us with other choices.

Thankfully, largely through our religious upbringing and the good examples of others, Kim and I have come to understand that the most fulfilling thing we can do with our lives is help other people. So we decided to give away the book advance money. As I mentioned briefly in chapter 1, we founded an organization called The Hope Effect.[4] Our goal with this nonprofit is to change orphan care around the world by providing solutions that mimic the family.

The need is almost too great to comprehend. There are an estimated 26 million children around the world who have lost both parents. And because orphanages can be impersonal and institutional, most of the orphans do not receive adequate personal interaction within a loving environment. Many kids who age out of orphanages are behind in every stage of development, only to face a future of crime, prostitution, or homelessness.

Through The Hope Effect, we are creating two-parent, family-style homes that provide opportunities for each child to flourish and thrive. We are offering real solutions to real problems.

What will become of this new endeavor? We don't know. It will undoubtedly grow and change over time. We'll make some mistakes. But we really believe that the net result will be better lives for a great many of the world's most vulnerable children.

And here's the truly amazing part: A significant part of the money for these projects is coming from the *Becoming Minimalist* community, those who follow my blog regularly. Minimalists are providing the resources! Ordinary men and women all around the world have decided their lives are better by owning less, and because they are not buying and caring for more stuff, they are free to use their resources to accomplish great things for others. In this case, they are literally providing families for children who desperately need them. Can you imagine the joy they are experiencing knowing the good they are accomplishing for others? I can, because I am experiencing it too.

I have shared the story of The Hope Effect with you, not because Kim and I are special, but *because we're so ordinary!* We never set out to accomplish anything like this. We just wanted to own less stuff. But once we did, our passions began to change and we could see pearls that now lay within our reach. If we can do something like this, anybody can. You can.

You certainly don't need to create your own nonprofit. You might choose instead to do something far less formal and organized. Go for it! That's just as good.

I know minimalists who have given up their personal possessions and as a result have found opportunities to open fair-trade businesses, become more involved in conservation research, donate to religious organizations, volunteer in their local communities, and help build a school in Laos. What are you going to do?

The important thing is to realize that you don't need to wait to begin. You already have influence. You already have opportunity. And you can start today right where you are.

EVERYDAY INFLUENCE

I believe that what I have been saying in this chapter has been resonating with you. You may already have been planning ways to be more useful to others, but even if not, the idea of it is now starting to excite you. Something deep within your soul says, *That's big. I want that.*

All of us crave to live lives of significance—lives that make a difference in the world around us. Each of us is born with an ingrained desire to live for something greater than ourselves.

You can see this all around us. Our world cares deeply about influence. We pay for it, fight for it, and study how to get more of it. Our world measures it, ranks it, and ascribes it to people for foolish reasons. But in our constant struggle to attain influence, we often miss out on one important truth.

We already have it! Each of us is already an influencer of others. In true minimalist style, we already have everything we need to make a difference in the life of someone else.

Whenever and wherever our lives intersect with the lives of others (at home, at work, online, or in our community), we have influence. We affect people every single day with the words we say, the looks on our faces, the actions we choose, and the decisions we make. Whether we interact with five people, fifty people, or five hundred people, our lives matter and produce ripple effects that extend far beyond us.

There are no neutral exchanges. Every interaction we have with another person can be positive or negative. We can add value to the lives of others, or we can drain it from them. Our opportunity for influence can become an important agent for change, or it can further cement the status quo. It can make our world a better place to be or a crummier place to endure.

Believe in the good you already have to offer. Be intentional about how you use your available influence.

Let's you and I and all minimalists remember that we already have what we need to influence others for the better and that we can start today. Let's celebrate growth, encourage strength, and push for positive change.

More and More

If minimalism enables you to have the life of leisure you want, I hope you'll enjoy it.

If you're looking forward to checking off some adventures on your bucket list, that's great.

If you've become more enamored of experiences than possessions, good for you. So have I.

Go for it. Chase your dreams with abandon. Removing your attachment to possessions will provide you with the freedom and opportunity to realize the life you've always wanted.

But if you really want to invest your minimalism dividend for maximum return, also use it to help others. Your family, people in your own community, and the poor and disadvantaged around the world need what you can give. And when you share freely with them, something wonderful will happen in your heart that no me-centered objective could ever provide.

Over time, I believe you'll get better and better at knowing how to do good effectively for others. I know that my wife and I have no intention of stopping our attempts at service with The Hope Effect. We think more ideas and opportunities for service will arise. And in the same way, I believe you can become devoted to service, wanting more and more of it and doing better and better at leveraging your influence.

This is the more of less. Our contribution to this world can be measured by something more meaningful than the size of our house, the car we drive, or the designer label on our jeans. Our lives are going to have lasting significance in how we choose to live them . . . and how we enable others to live theirs.

Dream big dreams for the one life you have been given.

Then wake up and live them.

Acknowledgments

During our first conversation, my agent, Chris Ferebee, asked me why I wanted to publish a book with a traditional publisher. As a blogger, I was used to having complete freedom over my work, and he knew that. But I already knew the answer before he even asked the question: "Chris, I want a publisher because I want to write a better book. With a team, this project will be better than if I do it alone. And this message is too important to not get it right the first time."

I knew what I wanted. But never, in my wildest dreams, did I imagine the amount of work, commitment, and dedication from others that would eventually go into making this book what it is today. It has been created not by me but by a team. And they deserve to be acknowledged.

I wish I could publically thank every person who played a role, big or small. Unfortunately, there are far too many and not enough space. However, some people do deserve special recognition for the investment they made into *The More of Less*.

Thank you to my editor and new friend, Eric Stanford, who has maybe spent more hours on this project than anyone else—sometimes I think even more than I have. Through countless reworks, e-mails, and phone conversations, you brought depth to my voice and words to my thoughts, and you created a book one thousand times better than I could have ever completed. From the bottom of my heart, thank you, Eric.

To my agent, Chris Ferebee, thank you for asking hard questions and pushing this book in the right direction from the very beginning. It exists because of you and I am forever grateful. Thank you for caring about me more than the project. And thank you for being a trustworthy voice throughout this process.

Thank you to my publisher, WaterBrook Multnomah. I sat on a chair in my bedroom closet for my first call with Susan Tjaden and David Kopp. By the time I hung up, I wanted no one else to publish this book. Your understanding of my passion, my voice, and my calling continue to be unparalleled. Thank you, Tina Constable, for speaking into this project from the very beginning and lending weight to its potential. Thank you, really, to the entire team at WaterBrook: the cover designers, the marketers, the copyeditors, the proofreaders, and so many more.

Thank you also to those who have modeled minimalism for me and shaped my view of it from the very beginning. Whether your words are quoted in this book or laid the foundation upon which it was written, your contribution can be found in these words and, equally so, in the life that I live.

A heartfelt thanks to *Becoming Minimalist* readers. Thank you for commenting on posts, sending e-mails, sharing content, and showing up at events. You make writing fun. Know that your encouragement has given me the motivation to stay up many late nights in front of a computer screen.

This journey began in Vermont and ended in Arizona, but my heart resides in South Dakota. I love my parents and my family more than I could ever express on paper. Thank you for believing in me and laying a foundation for my life built on character and trust, peace and perseverance, grace and love.

Finally, and most importantly, thank you to my faithful wife, Kimberly, and my beautiful children, Salem and Alexa. Your love and laughter bring joy to my life, a skip to my step, and greater inspiration to my work. I am proud of this book but prouder of you. May the world be blessed through the lives that you live.

And may all of us find greater pursuits than material possessions.

Notes

Chapter 1: Becoming Minimalist

1. Will Rogers, BrainyQuote.com, www.brainyquote.com/quotes/quotes/w/willrogers167212.html.

2. James Twitchell, "Two Cheers for Materialism," *The Consumer Society Reader,* eds. Juliet Schor and D. B. Holt (New York: W. W. Norton, 2000), 283.

3. Mary MacVean, "For Many People, Gathering Possessions Is Just the Stuff of Life," *Los Angeles Times,* March 21, 2014, http://articles.latimes.com/2014/mar/21/health/la-he-keeping-stuff-20140322.

4. "Average Home Has More TVs Than People," *USA Today,* September 21, 2006, http://usatoday30.usatoday.com/life/television/news/2006-09-21-homes-tv_x.htm.

5. National Association of Professional Organizers, www.napo.net/press_room/organizing_statistics.pdf.

6. "UPPERcase Inc. Outlook on Residential Storage," UPPERcase Modular Storage Systems, http://uppercasestorage.com/cmsdocs/Whitepaper_on_Residential_Storage_Market.pdf.

7. Jon Mooallem, "The Self-Storage Self," *New York Times Magazine,* September 2, 2009, www.nytimes.com/2009/09/06/magazine/06self-storage-t.html?_r=0.

8. Tim Chen, "American Household Credit Card Debt Statistics: 2015," NerdWallet.com, www.nerdwallet.com/blog/credit-card-data/average-credit-card-debt-household/.

9. Louise Story, "Anywhere the Eye Can See, It's Likely to See an Ad," *New York Times,* January 15, 2007, www.nytimes.com/2007/01/15/business/media/15everywhere.html?_r=0.

Chapter 2: Good Riddance

1. Luke 18:18, 22–23, MSG.

2. John 10:10, MSG.

3. See Changing Times: Holistic Journalism That Makes a Difference, https://time2transcend.wordpress.com/.

Chapter 3: Minimalism Your Way

1. These people are all my fellow bloggers. Dave Bruno: http://guynameddave .com/. Colin Wright: http://exilelifestyle.com/. Tammy Strobel: http:// tammystrobel.com/. Leo Babauta: http://zenhabits.net/. Francine Jay: www.missminimalist.com. Everett Bogue: http://evbogue.com/. Karen Kingston: www.karenkingston.com. Adam Baker: http://manvsdebt.com/.
2. Mark 5:18–19, MSG.
3. Dave Balthrop, "The Trip That Changed Everything," *SimpleLifeReboot,* http://simplelifereboot.com/the-trip-that-changed-everything/; and "Our Journey," http://simplelifereboot.com/about-us/our-journey/.

Chapter 4: The Fog of Consumerism

1. Ernest Dichter, quoted in Sarah van Gelder, "A Brief History of Happiness: How America Lost Track of the Good Life—and Where to Find It Now," *Yes! Magazine,* February 5, 2015, www.yesmagazine.org/happiness /how-america-lost-track-of-the-good-life-and-where-to-find-it-now. I am indebted to Van Gelder's article for her analysis of the history of American consumerism.
2. Van Gelder, "A Brief History of Happiness."
3. "Song Dong," Museum of Modern Art, www.moma.org/interactives /exhibitions/projects/song-dong/.
4. One of many resources on the generations is Jill Novak, "The Six Living Generations in America," The Marketing Teacher, May 8, 2014, www .marketingteacher.com/the-six-living-generations-in-america/.
5. Derek Thompson and Jordan Weissman, "The Cheapest Generation: Why Millennials Aren't Buying Cars or Houses, and What That Means for the Economy," *Atlantic,* September 2012, www.theatlantic.com/magazine /archive/2012/09/the-cheapest-generation/309060/.
6. Kevin Tampone, "Black Friday 2014: By the Numbers," Syracuse.com, November 26, 2014, www.syracuse.com/news/index.ssf/2014/11/black _friday_2014_by_the_numbers.html.
7. "US Total Media Ad Spend Inches Up, Pushed by Digital," eMarketer.com, August 22, 2013, www.emarketer.com/Article/ US-Total-Media-Ad-Spend-Inches-Up-Pushed-by-Digital/1010154.
8. Drazen Prelec and Duncan Simester, "Always Leave Home Without It: A Further Investigation of the Credit-Card Effect on Willingness to Pay," *Marketing Letters* 12, no. 1 (February 2001): 1, 5–12, http://link.springer .com/article/10.1023/A%3A1008196717017.

9. Brad Tuttle, "J.C. Penney's Pricing Is Faker Than Ever," *Time,* January 31, 2014, http://business.time.com/2014/01/31/j-c-penneys-pricing-is-faker-than-ever/.

10. Carrie Sloan, "9 Secret Ways Stores Seduce Us into Buying," LearnVest.com, September 23, 2011, www.learnvest.com/knowledge-center/9-secret-ways-stores-seduce-us-into-buying/.

Chapter 5: The Want Within

1. Margaret S. Clark et al., "Heightened Interpersonal Security Diminishes the Monetary Value of Possessions," *Journal of Experimental Social Psychology* 47, no. 2 (March 2011): 359–64, quoted in Serena Gordon, "Insecurity in Relationships Binds People to Possessions," *US News and World Report,* March 11, 2011, http://health.usnews.com/health-news/family-health/brain-and-behavior/articles/2011/03/11/insecurity-in-relationships-binds-people-to-possessions.

Chapter 6: Take It Easy

1. Joshua Fields Millburn, "Does This Add Value to My Life?," *The Minimalists,* www.theminimalists.com/add-value/.

2. Marie Kondo, *The Life-Changing Magic of Tidying Up: The Japanese Art of Decluttering and Organizing,* trans. Cathy Hirano (Berkeley, CA: Ten Speed Press, 2014), 39.

3. Peter Walsh, interview by Linda Samuels, "Ask the Expert: Peter Walsh," *The Other Side of Organized,* May 21, 2013, http://theothersideoforganized.com/blog/2013/5/21/ask-the-expert-peter-walsh.html.

4. William Morris, BrainyQuote.com, www.brainyquote.com/quotes/quotes/w/williammor158643.html.

Chapter 7: Troubleshooting

1. Dave Bruno, *The 100 Thing Challenge: How I Got Rid of Almost Everything, Remade My Life, and Regained My Soul* (New York: Harper, 2010), 80.

2. Bruno, *The 100 Thing Challenge,* 81–82.

3. Bruno, *The 100 Thing Challenge,* 76, 81–82, 85.

4. National Association of Professional Organizers, www.napo.net/press_room/organizing_statistics.pdf, 9.

5. Michael F. Woolery, *Seize the Day! How to Best Use What Can't Be Replaced — Time* (Oklahoma City: TimeLink, 1991), 89.

6. Leo Babauta, "Clutter Is Procrastination," *mnmlist,* http://mnmlist.com/clutter-is-procrastination/.

7. John Patrick Pullen, "How to Go Completely Paperless This Year," *Time,* January 19, 2015, http://time.com/3672824/go-paperless/.

8. Internal Revenue Service, "How Long Should I Keep Records?," www.irs.gov/Businesses/Small-Businesses-&-Self-Employed/How-long-should-I-keep-records.

9. Erin Stepp, "Annual Cost to Own and Operate a Vehicle Falls to $8,698, Finds AAA," American Automobile Association, April 28, 2015, http://newsroom.aaa.com/2015/04/annual-cost-operate-vehicle-falls-8698-finds-aaa/.

10. Phil LeBeau, "Americans Borrowing Record Amount to Buy Cars," CNBC, March 4, 2014, www.cnbc.com/id/101461972.

11. Harvey Mackay, Twitter, January 29, 2013, https://twitter.com/harveymackay/status/296293630627438592.

Chapter 8: Experiments in Living with Less

1. See http://patrickrhone.com/.

2. Patrick Rhone, *Enough* (First Today Press, 2012), 10–11.

3. See http://bemorewithless.com/.

4. See http://theproject333.com/.

5. See www.theminimalists.com.

6. Ryan Nicodemus, "Packing Party: Unpack a Simpler Life," *The Minimalists,* www.theminimalists.com/packing/.

7. Ryan Nicodemus, from an earlier version of "Day 8, Beliefs," *The Minimalists,* www.theminimalists.com/21days/day8/.

8. See 1 Kings 10:14–29.

9. Ecclesiastes 2:1.

10. Ecclesiastes 2:4–9.

11. Ecclesiastes 2:10.

12. Ecclesiastes 2:11.

Chapter 9: Maintenance Program

1. Sarah Peck, "The Story of Enough: Giving Up (New) Clothes for One Year," guest post, *Becoming Minimalist,* www.becomingminimalist.com/minimalist-enough/.

2. Katy Wolk-Stanley, "Why I've Chosen to Buy Nothing New for 8 Years," guest post, *Money Saving Mom,* August 3, 2015, http://moneysavingmom

.com/2015/08/ive-chosen-buy-nothing-new-8-years.html. See Katy's website at http://thenonconsumeradvocate.com/.

3. Assya Barrette, "7 Eye-Opening Lessons I Learned from Buying Nothing New for 200 Days," Collective Evolution, August 19, 2015, www .collective-evolution.com/2015/08/19/7-eye-opening-lessons-i-learned -from-buying-nothing-new-for-200-days/.

4. Cait Flanders, "The Year I Embraced Minimalism and Completed a Yearlong Shopping Ban," Blonde on a Budget, July 6, 2015, http://blondeonabudget .ca/2015/07/06/the-year-i-embraced-minimalism-and-completed-a-yearlong -shopping-ban/.

5. Jeff Shinabarger, "147 Meals Later," *Huffington Post,* December 28, 2012, www.huffingtonpost.com/jeff-shinabarger/147-meals-later_b_2362892.html.

6. "Recent Holiday Shopping Trends," Fundivo, from the National Retail Federation, www.fundivo.com/stats/retail-holiday-shopping-statistics/.

7. "Giving Thanks Can Make You Happier," HEALTHbeat, Nov. 22, 2011, www.health.harvard.edu/healthbeat/giving-thanks-can-make-you-happier.

8. Emily L. Polak and Michael E. McCullough, "Is Gratitude an Alternative to Materialism?," *Journal of Happiness Studies 7,* no. 3 (September 2006): 355.

Chapter 10: The Minimalist Family

1. See www.minimalstudent.com.

Chapter 11: Shortcut to Significance

1. Matthew 6:21.

2. See http://withthisring.org/.

3. "Charitable Giving in America: Some Facts and Figures," National Center for Charitable Statistics, http://nccs.urban.org/nccs/statistics/Charitable -Giving-in-America-Some-Facts-and-Figures.cfm; "Charitable Giving Statistics," National Philanthropic Trust, www.nptrust.org/philanthropic -resources/charitable-giving-statistics/; and "Giving USA 2015: Annual Report on Philanthropy for the Year 2014," Giving USA, http://givingusa .org/product/giving-usa-2015-report-highlights/.

4. Anne Frank, *Anne Frank's Tales from the Secret Annex* (New York: Bantam, 2003), 89.

5. One of many sources confirming that being generous and compassionate is good for your health is Jeanie Lerche Davis, "The Science of Good Deeds," WebMD, www.webmd.com/balance/features/science-good-deeds.

6. Susan Adams, "Guess What Stresses Americans the Most," *Forbes,*

February 4, 2015, www.forbes.com/sites/susanadams/2015/02/04 /guess-what-stresses-americans-the-most/.

7. "The World of Seven Billion," *National Geographic,* http://ngm .nationalgeographic.com/2011/03/age-of-man/map-interactive.

Chapter 12: An Intentional Life

1. "Three-Quarters of Parents Too Busy to Read Bedtime Stories," *Telegraph* (UK), February 27, 2009, www.telegraph.co.uk/women/mother -tongue/4839894/Three-quarters-of-parents-too-busy-to-read-bedtime -stories.html.

2. Dean Schabner, "Americans: Overworked, Overstressed," ABC News, http:// abcnews.go.com/US/story?id=93604&page=1&singlePage=true.

3. A. Pawlowski, "Why Is America the 'No-Vacation Nation'?," CNN, May 23, 2011, www.cnn.com/2011/TRAVEL/05/23/vacation.in.america/index .html?_s=PM:TRAVEL.

4. Report highlights, "Stress in America: Paying with Our Health," American Psychological Association, www.apa.org/news/press/releases/stress/2014 /highlights.aspx, full article at www.apa.org/news/press/releases/stress/2014 /stress-report.pdf.

5. Mike Burns, "5 Steps to Declutter Your Schedule and Live Your Desired Life," guest blog, *Becoming Minimalist,* www.becomingminimalist.com/declutter -your-schedule/. Mike blogs at http://theothersideofcomplexity.com/.

6. Lucius Annaeus Seneca, *On the Shortness of Life* (London: William Heinemann, 1932), part VII, https://en.wikisource.org/wiki/On_the _shortness_of_life/Chapter_VII.

7. "The American Society for Aesthetic Plastic Surgery Reports Americans Spent Largest Amount on Cosmetic Surgery Since the Great Recession of 2008," news release, American Society for Aesthetic Plastic Surgery, March 20, 2014, www.surgery.org/media/news-releases/the-american-society-for -aesthetic-plastic-surgery-reports-americans-spent-largest-amount-on -cosmetic-surger; and "Statistics and Facts on the Cosmetics Industry," Statista.com, www.statista.com/topics/1008/cosmetics-industry/.

8. Melissa Dahl, "Stop Obsessing: Women Spend 2 Weeks a Year on Their Appearance, TODAY Survey Shows," *Today,* February 24, 2014, www.today .com/health/stop-obsessing-women-spend-2-weeks-year-their-appearance -today-2D12104866.

9. Lucy Waterlow, "He's the Fairest of Them All! Men Now Spend Longer on Grooming and Getting Ready Than Women," *Daily Mail* (UK), January 25, 2013, www.dailymail.co.uk/femail/article-2268214/HEs-fairest-Men -spend-longer-grooming-getting-ready-women.html.

10. Emma Johnson, "The Real Cost of Your Shopping Habits," *Forbes,* January 15, 2015, www.forbes.com/sites/emmajohnson/2015/01/15/the-real-cost -of-your-shopping-habits/.

11. Johnson, "The Real Cost of Your Shopping Habits."

12. Mattias Wallander, "Closet Cast-offs Clogging Landfills," *Huffington Post,* June 27, 2010, www.huffingtonpost.com/mattias-wallander/closet-cast-offs -clogging_b_554400.html.

13. Dahl, "Stop Obsessing."

14. Olga Khazan, "Why Do So Many Women Wear So Much Makeup?" *Atlantic,* April 28, 2014, www.theatlantic.com/health/archive/2014/04 /women-wear-too-much-makeup-because-they-mistakenly-think-men-want -them-to/361264/.

15. "Overweight and Obesity Statistics," National Institute of Diabetes and Digestive and Kidney Diseases, October 2012, www.niddk.nih.gov /health-information/health-statistics/Pages/overweight-obesity-statistics .aspx.

16. "One in Five Adults Meet Overall Physical Activity Guidelines," press release, Centers for Disease Control and Prevention, May 2, 2013, www.cdc.gov /media/releases/2013/p0502-physical-activity.html.

17. "Fast Food Statistics," Statistic Brain Research Institute, www.statisticbrain. com/fast-food-statistics/; and David Hinckley, "Americans Spend 34 Hours a Week Watching Television, According to Nielsen Numbers," *New York Daily News,* September 19, 2012, www.nydailynews.com/entertainment /tv-movies/americans-spend-34-hours-week-watching-tv-nielsen-numbers -article-1.1162285.

18. Gary Thomas, *Every Body Matters: Strengthening Your Body to Strengthen Your Soul* (Grand Rapids, MI: Zondervan, 2011), 15.

19. "Water: How Much Should You Drink Every Day?" Mayo Clinic, September 5, 2014, www.mayoclinic.org/healthy-lifestyle/nutrition-and-healthy-eating /in-depth/water/art-20044256.

20. "How Much Physical Activity Do Adults Need?," Centers for Disease Control and Prevention, June 4, 2015, www.cdc.gov/physicalactivity/basics /adults/.

Chapter 13: Don't Settle for Less

1. Matthew 13:45–46.
2. Philip Moeller, "Why Helping Others Makes Us Happy," *US News & World Report,* April 4, 2012, http://money.usnews.com/money/personal-finance/articles/2012/04/04/why-helping-others-makes-us-happy.
3. Rabindranath Tagore, BrainyQuote.com, www.brainyquote.com/quotes/quotes/r/rabindrana134933.html.
4. See http://hopeeffect.com/.

About the Author

Joshua Becker is one of the leading voices in the modern simplicity movement. He is the founder and editor of *Becoming Minimalist,* a website dedicated to intentional living, visited by over one million readers every month. He is, in addition, an accomplished international speaker whose story has appeared in *Time, Success,* the *Wall Street Journal,* the *Boston Globe, Christianity Today,* the *Guardian* (UK), and many other publications. He wrote the *Wall Street Journal*–best-selling book *Simplify* and also *Clutterfree with Kids.*

With his wife, Kim, Joshua is also a founder of The Hope Effect, a nonprofit organization dedicated to changing how the world cares for orphans by focusing on family-based solutions.

Joshua holds a bachelor of science degree in business administration from the University of Nebraska at Omaha and a master's degree in theological studies from Bethel Seminary in St. Paul, Minnesota. He served for fifteen years in pastoral ministry at churches in Nebraska, Wisconsin, Vermont, and Arizona. Currently, he lives near Phoenix, Arizona, with his wife and two children.

becomingminimalist.com

Becoming Minimalist inspires others to live more by owning less. The website is home to over 1 million readers per month who recognize life is too valuable to waste chasing material possessions.

With encouragement, inspiration, and practical advice, it encourages each reader to discover the life-giving benefits of owning less.

— —

Need a little help owning less? *Uncluttered* is a 12-week, self-guided, online course designed to help you own less, live more, and discover the life you've always wanted.

The program includes videos, interviews, articles, weekly challenges, and an engaged community—all packaged to help you declutter your home and start living a better life.

Find out more at my.becomingminimalist.com. And use code: BOOK25 for a 25% discount.

— —

#THEMOREOFLESS